AF395682

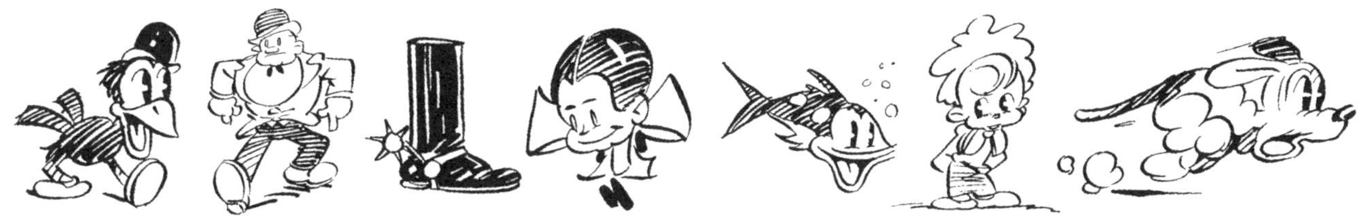

HOW TO CLASSIC DRAW CARTOONS

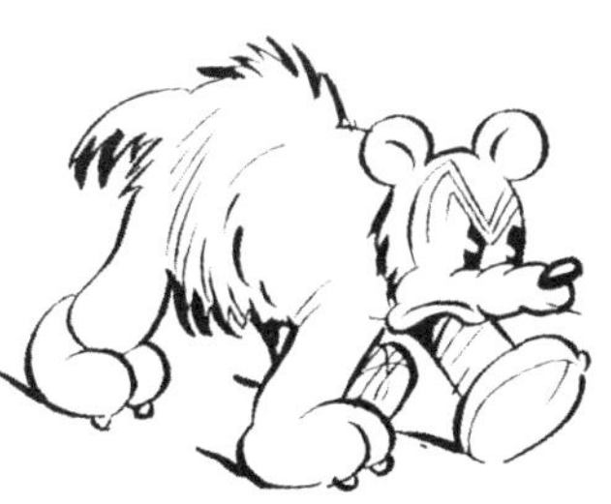
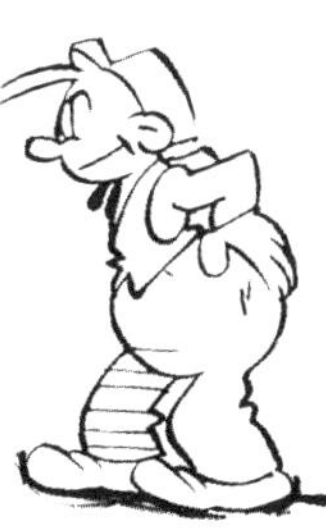
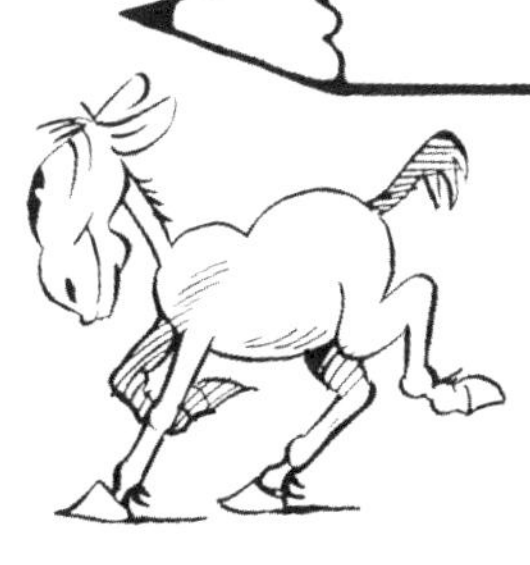
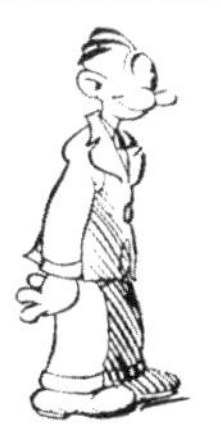
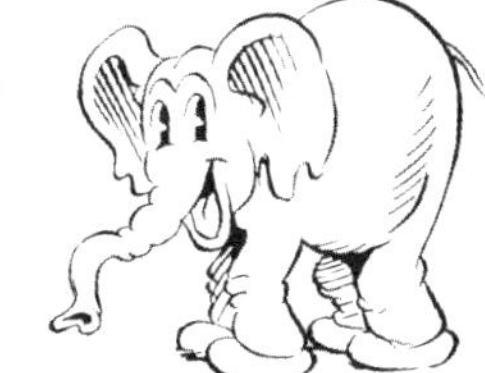

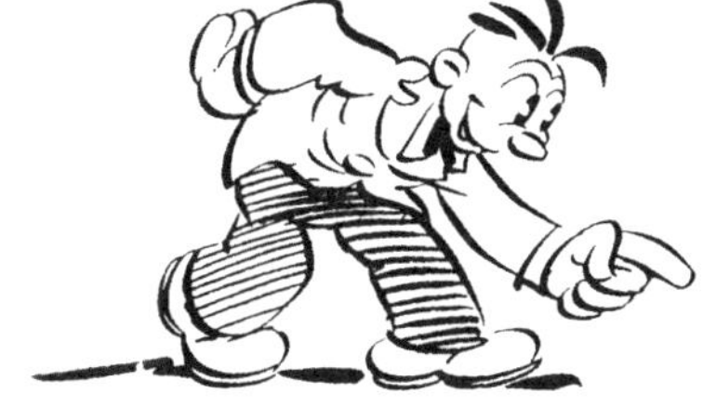

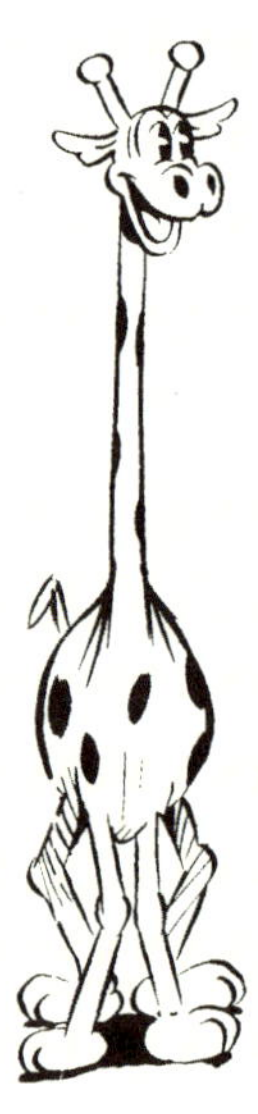

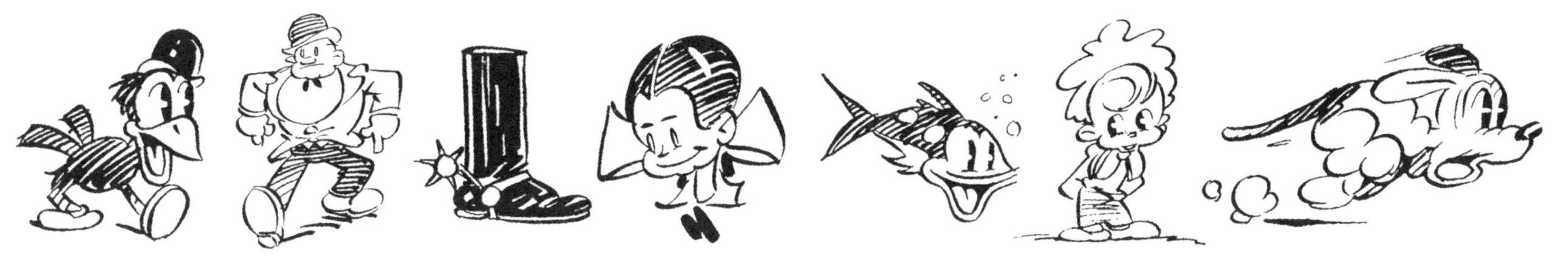

HOW TO DRAW CLASSIC CARTOONS

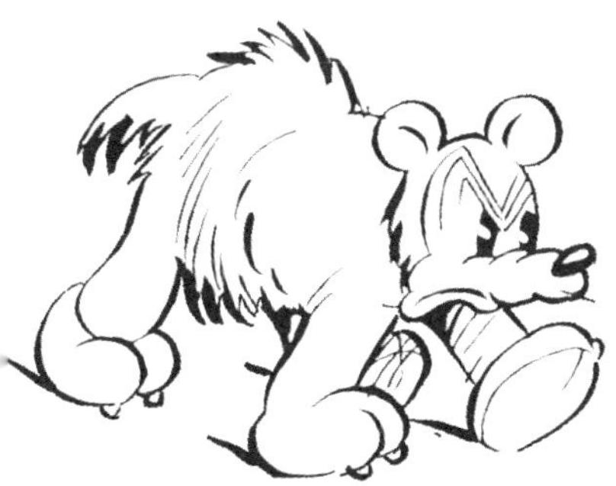

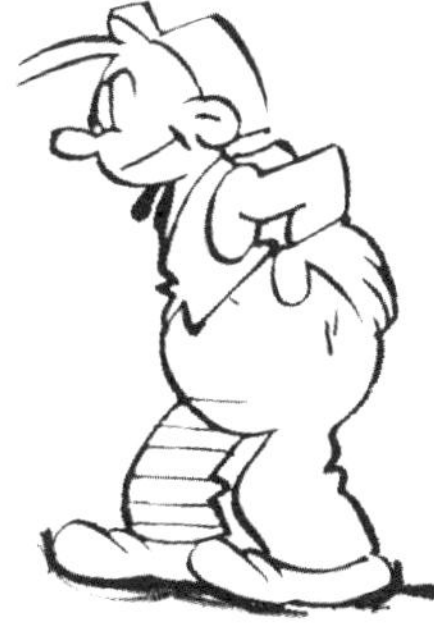

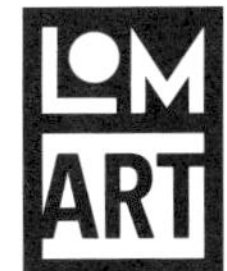

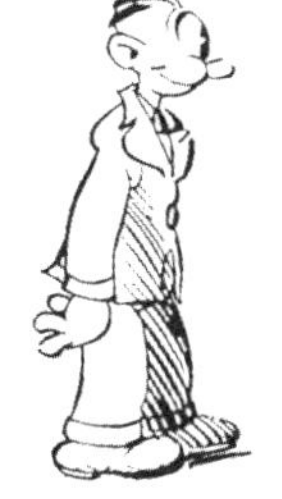

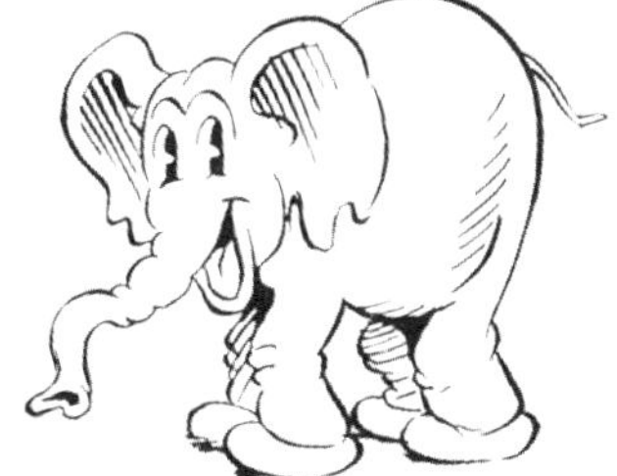

Introduction

American artist and director Bill Nolan pioneered the iconic "rubber hose"
style of animation used in 1920s cartoons such as Felix the Cat, Betty Boop,
and Popeye.

Instantly recognizable from its curved lines and the elastic-like movements
of its animated characters (hence the name "rubber hose"), this distinctive
style can be easily recreated using simple circles as a starting point.

The step-by-step guides and words of advice on the pages that follow
were first published back in 1936, but remain just as enlightening today.
With just a little practice, and a few helpful hints from Nolan himself,
you'll be creating your own classic cartoons in no time.

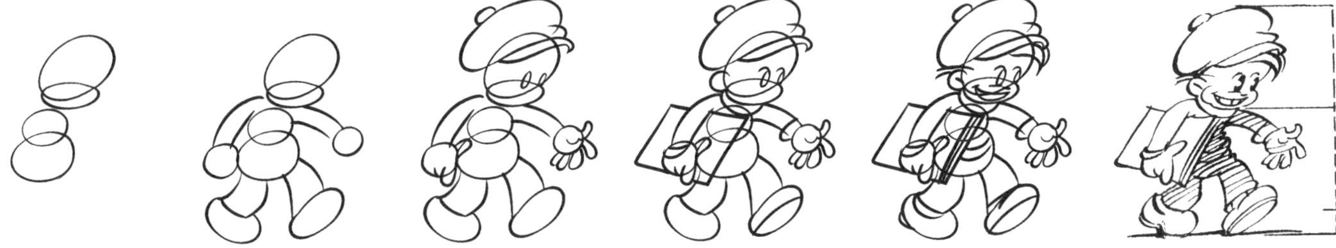

Strokes

The materials necessary for making pen and ink comics are few. A drawing pen, paper
that will accept the ink, a pen, pencil, and an eraser are all that are absolutely necessary.

A common breadboard will serve for a drawing board, but if one is not available,
a smooth-topped table will suffice. Thumb tacks to hold the paper on the board
are convenient.

Comics are first laid out in lead pencil and then inked in. When the ink dries,
the pencil lines can be removed with an eraser without injury to the ink lines.

Ability to handle a pen is acquired only by practice. The exercises on the opposite
page are to be practiced until you are able to accomplish the strokes with sureness
and confidence. At first, practice the strokes slowly, being careful that the lines do
not run together. When you get the feel of the pen, increase the speed of your stroke.
The arrows indicate the direction in which the pen travels.

When you have mastered the various strokes, make simple landscapes, like the one
on the right of the page, using different types of lines to get the various tones.

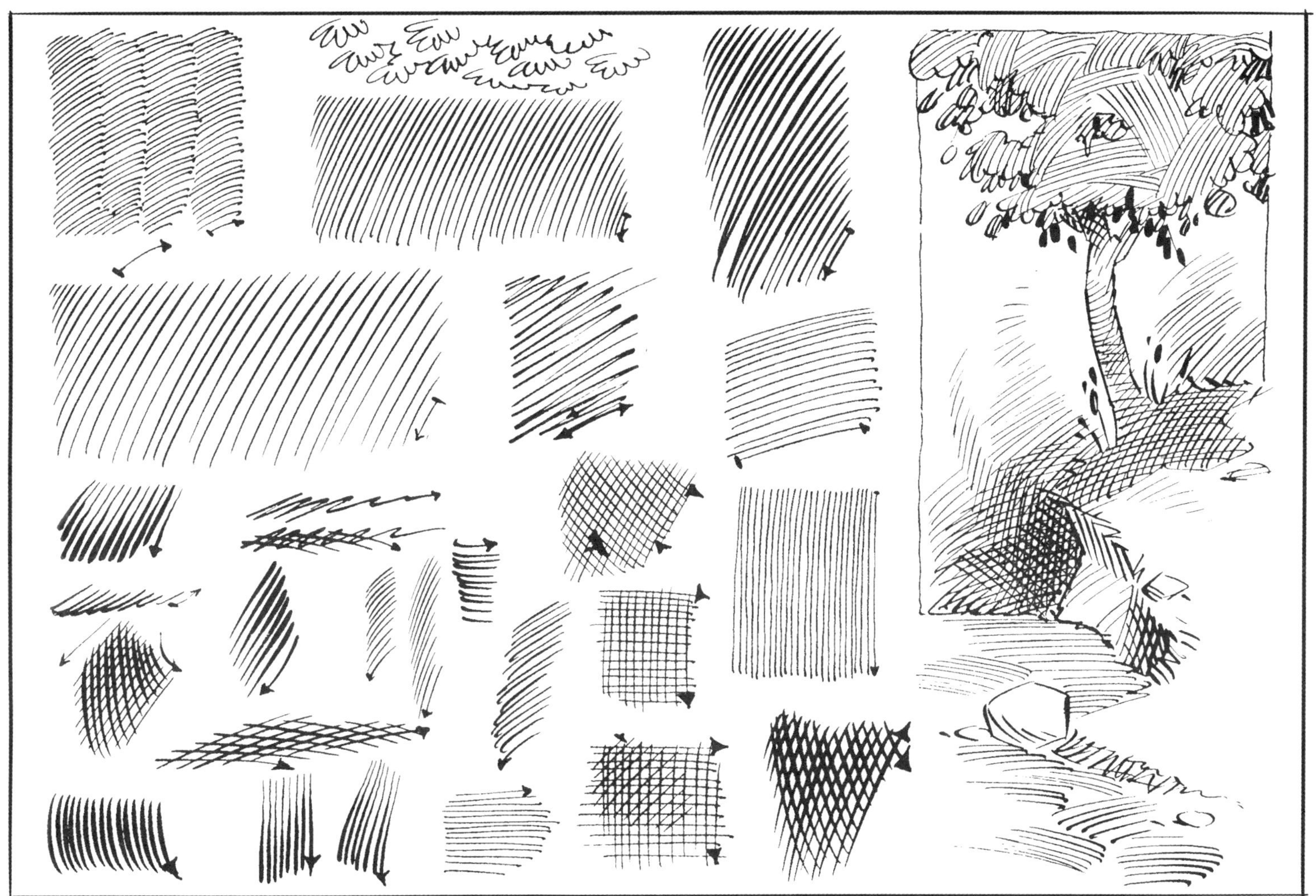

The Hands

In the boxes on the opposite page, you will notice that the first of each series of three drawings is a rough circle. In starting to draw the hand, always make this circle in pencil. It represents the center of the hand, either the palm or the back, on to which you attach the thumb and fingers.

The second drawing in each box shows the thumb and fingers drawn over the original circle. This is also done in pencil. When the drawing is inked in, those parts of the pencil drawing which are not wanted in the finished picture are left out, as you will see has been done in the third pictures in the boxes.

Study the hands and note how the fingers and thumb are attached to suggest a certain pose. Bear in mind that in drawing comics you merely suggest, and do not go into detail, as is done in illustrating.

Using the following pages as a guide, practice making hands until you are able to draw them in any desired position. This will require patience, but you can do it.

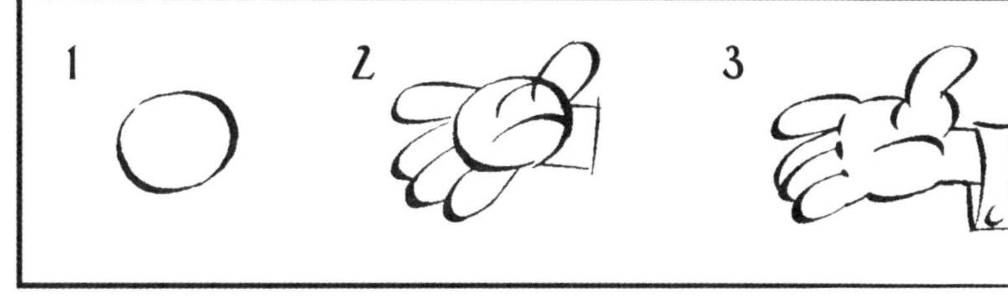

1
2
3

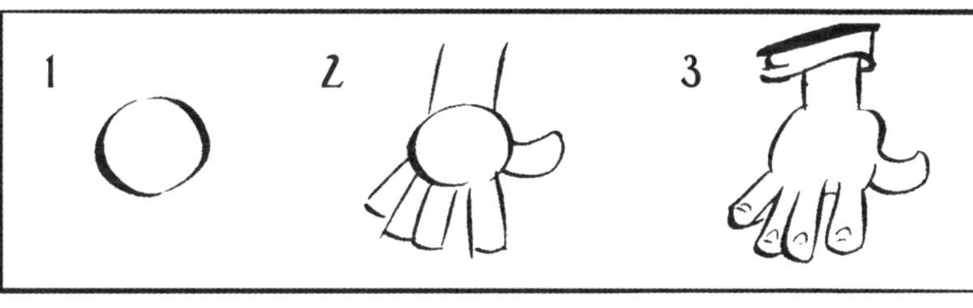

1
2
3

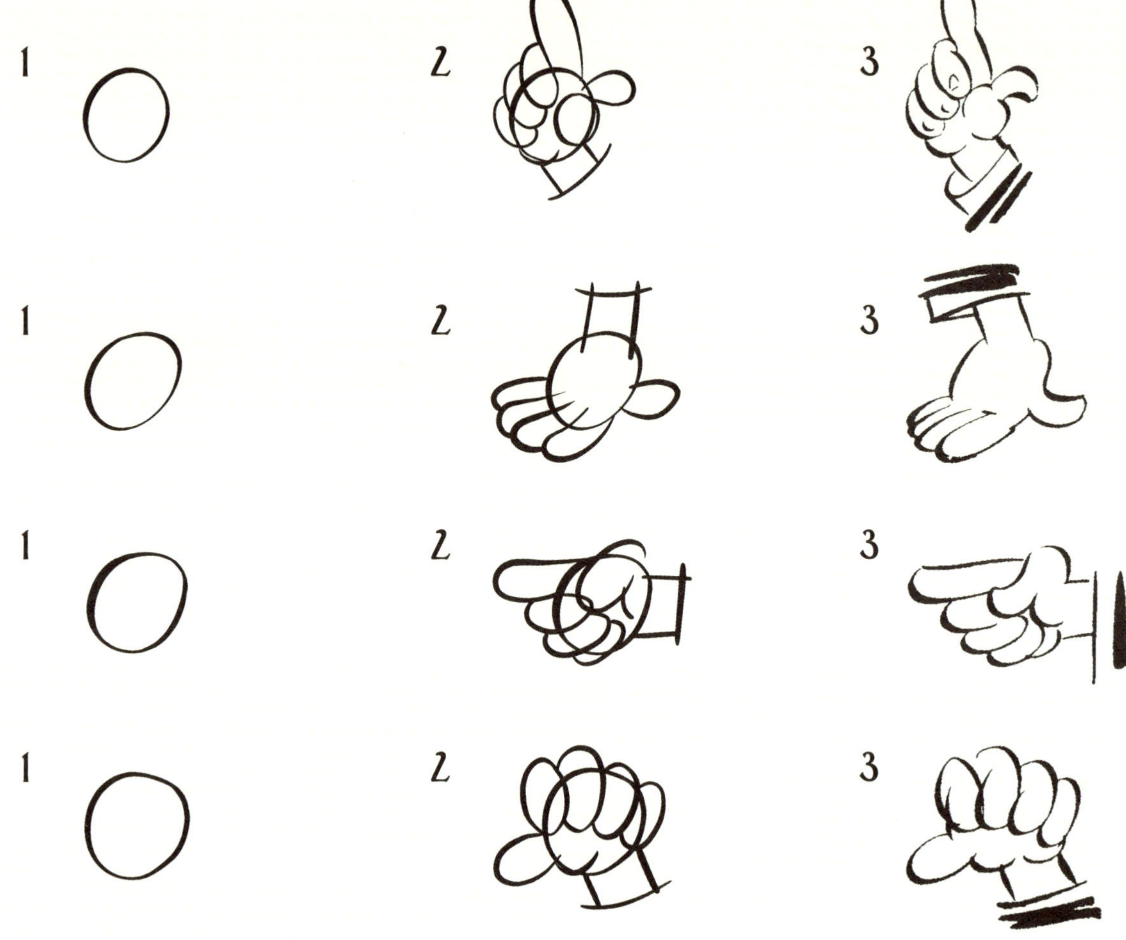

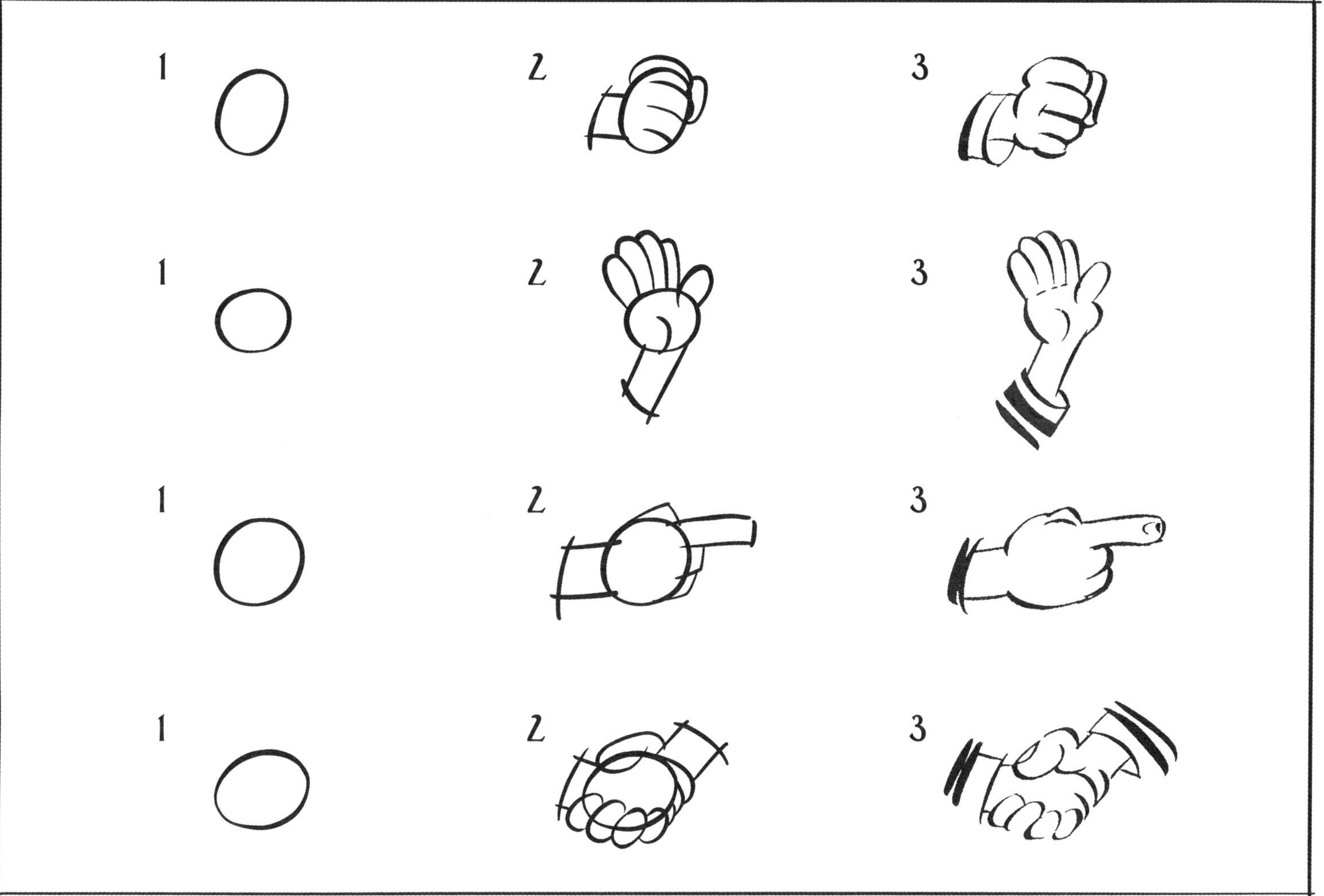

1
2
3
1
2
3
1
2
3
1
2
3

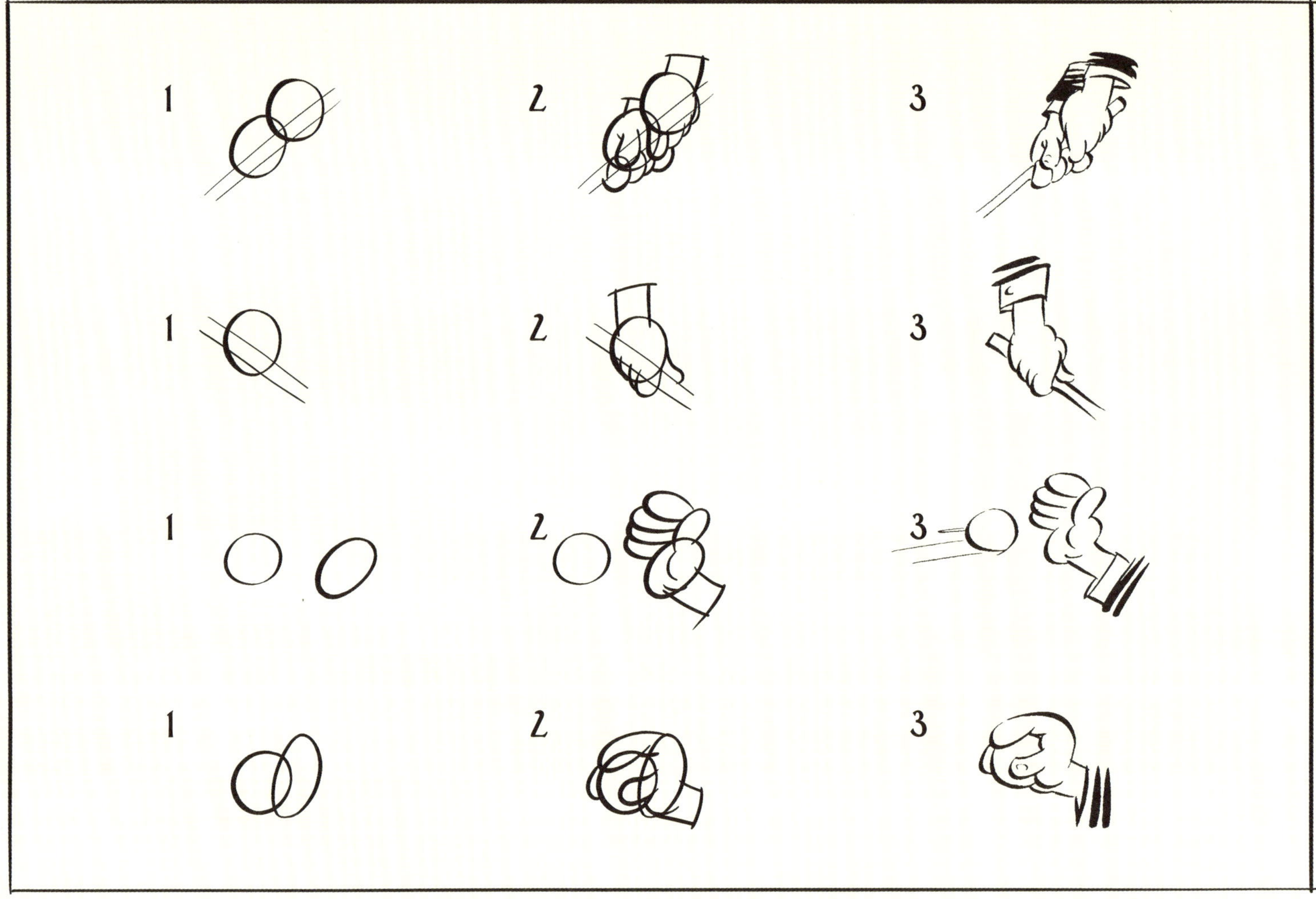

1
2
3
1
2
3
1
2
3
1
2
3

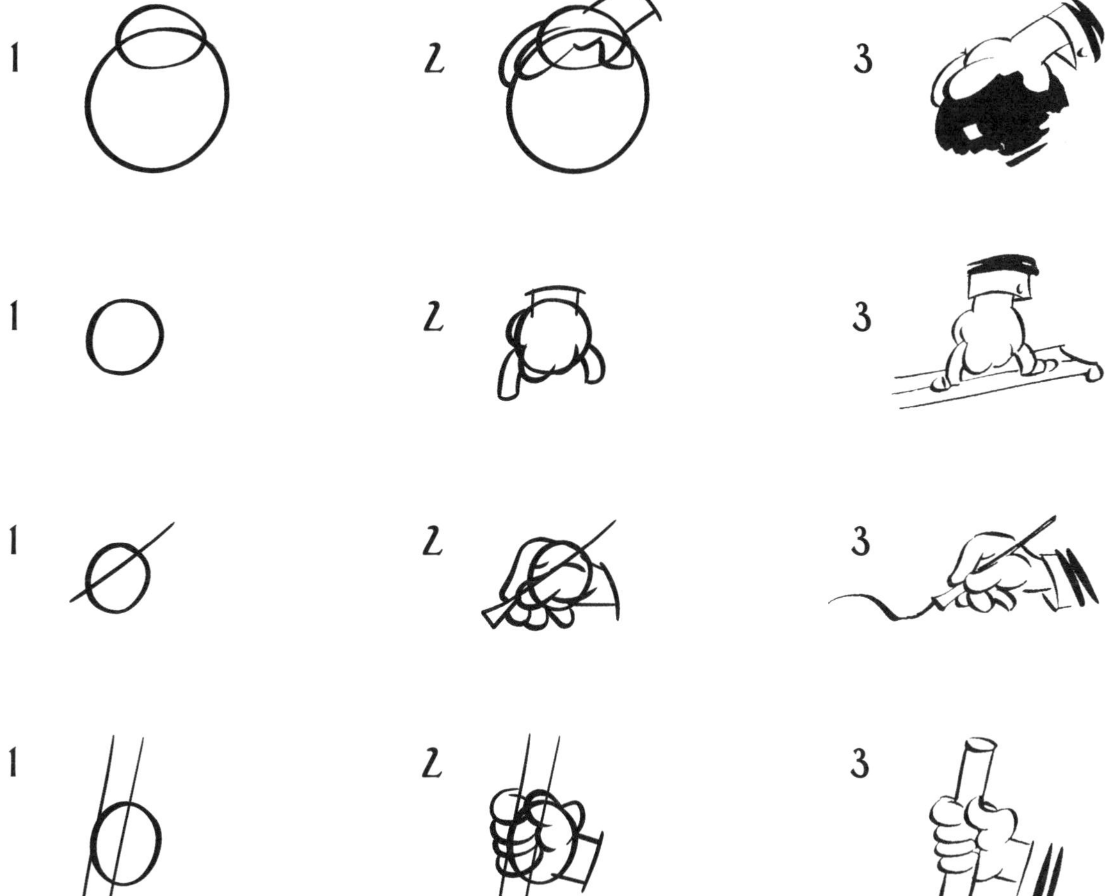

1
2
3
1
2
3
1
2
3
1
2
3

The Feet

Study the drawings opposite and then make up a page of shoes from your imagination.

It is necessary to be able to draw a variety of shoes, because each comic figure demands a type of shoe that fits the character. A business person needs smart shoes; a dude requires shoes with spats; a farmer, boots; and so on down the line.

In making buttoned shoes, be sure the buttons are on the outside of the foot. This is true, also, of spats.

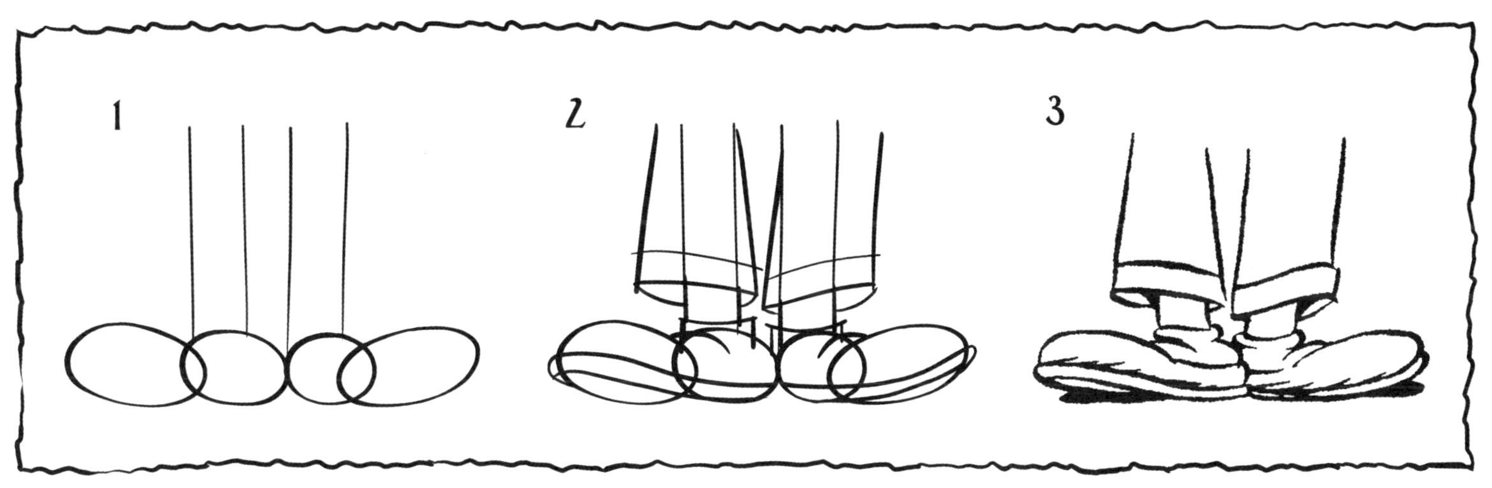
1
2
3

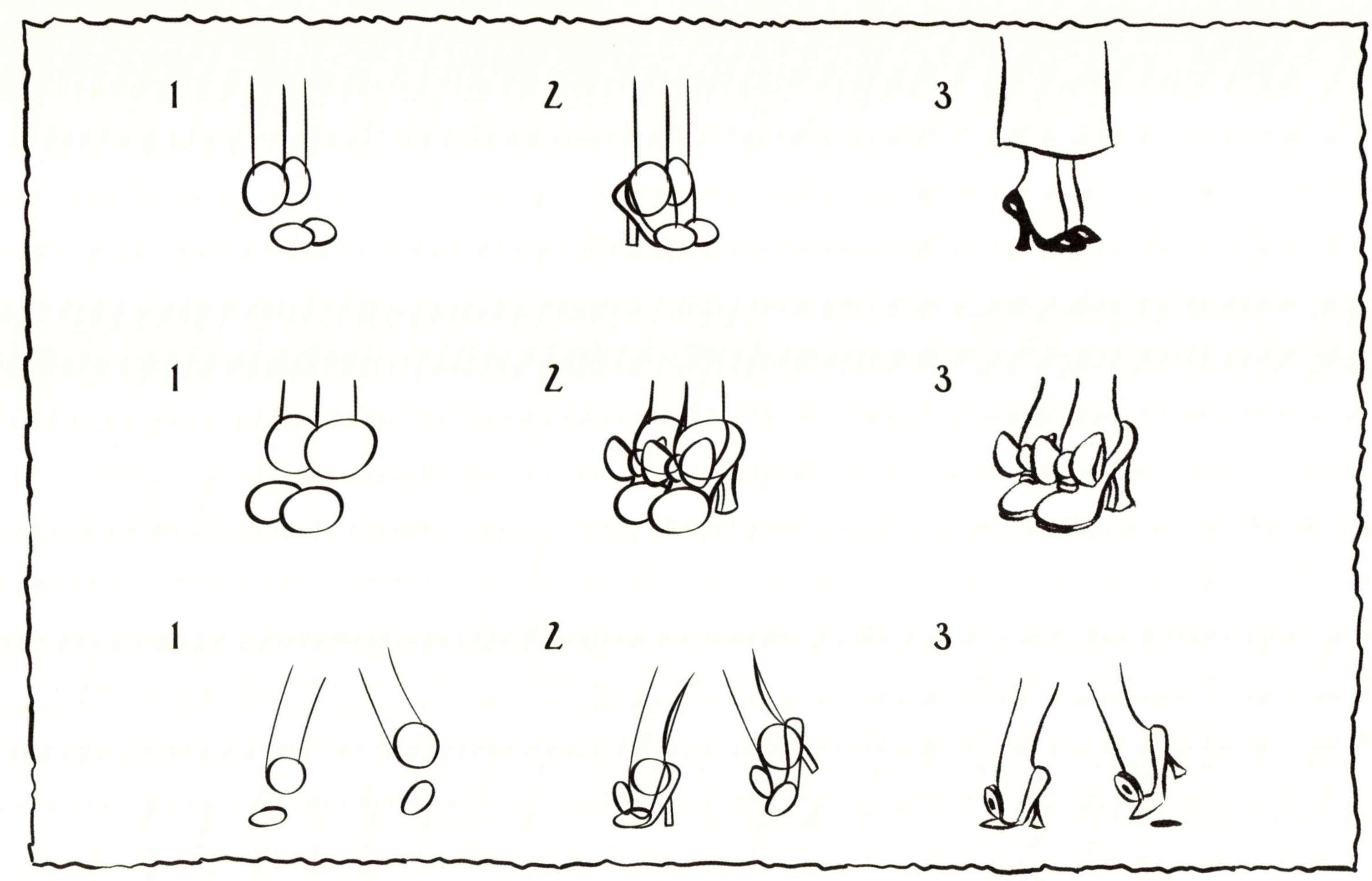

1
2
3
1
2
3
1
2
3

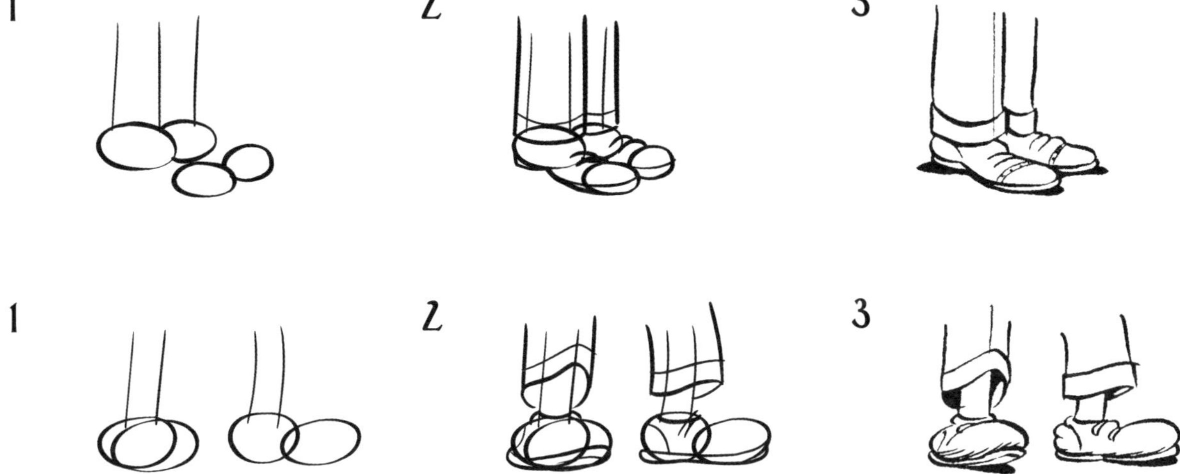

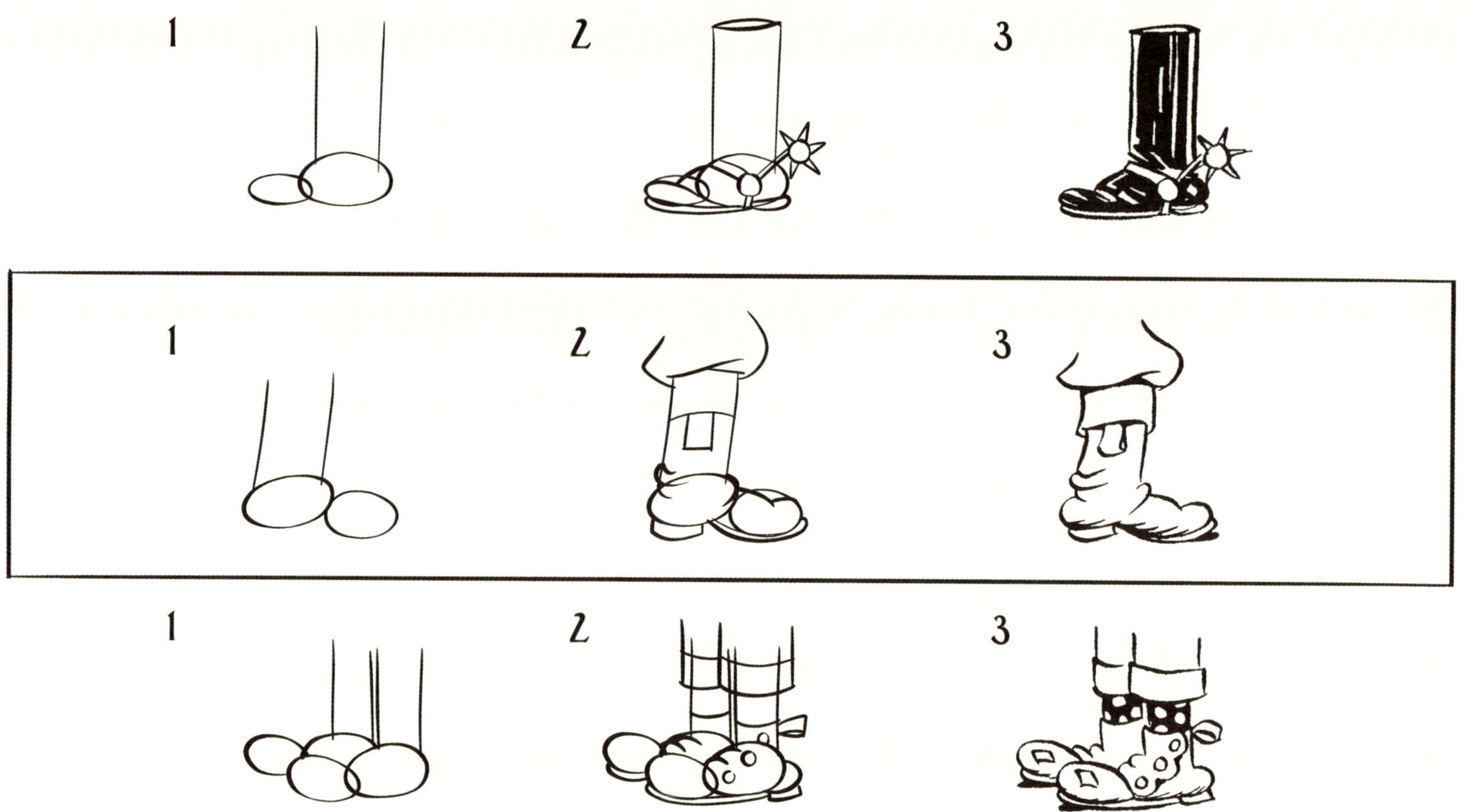
1
2
3
1
2
3
1
2
3

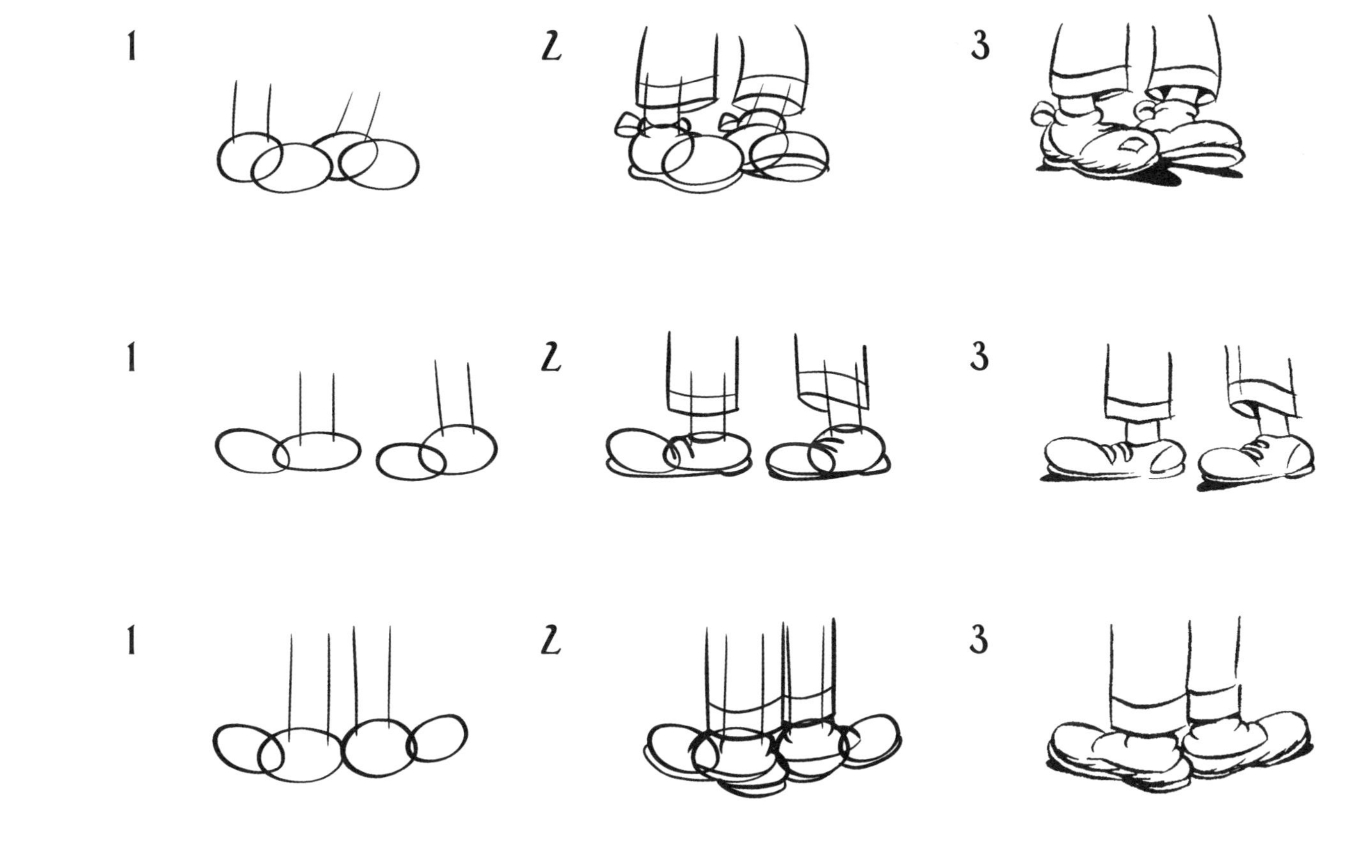

1
2
3
1
2
3
1
2
3

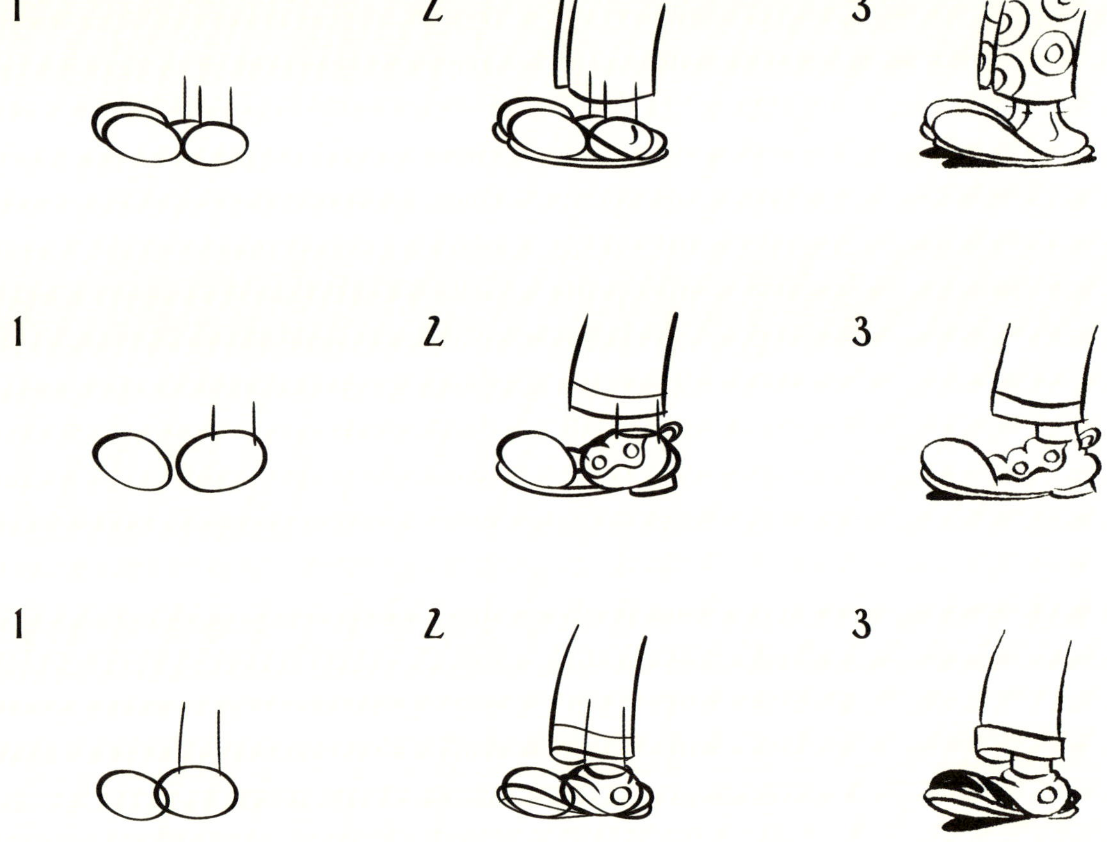

1
2
3
1
2
3
1
2
3

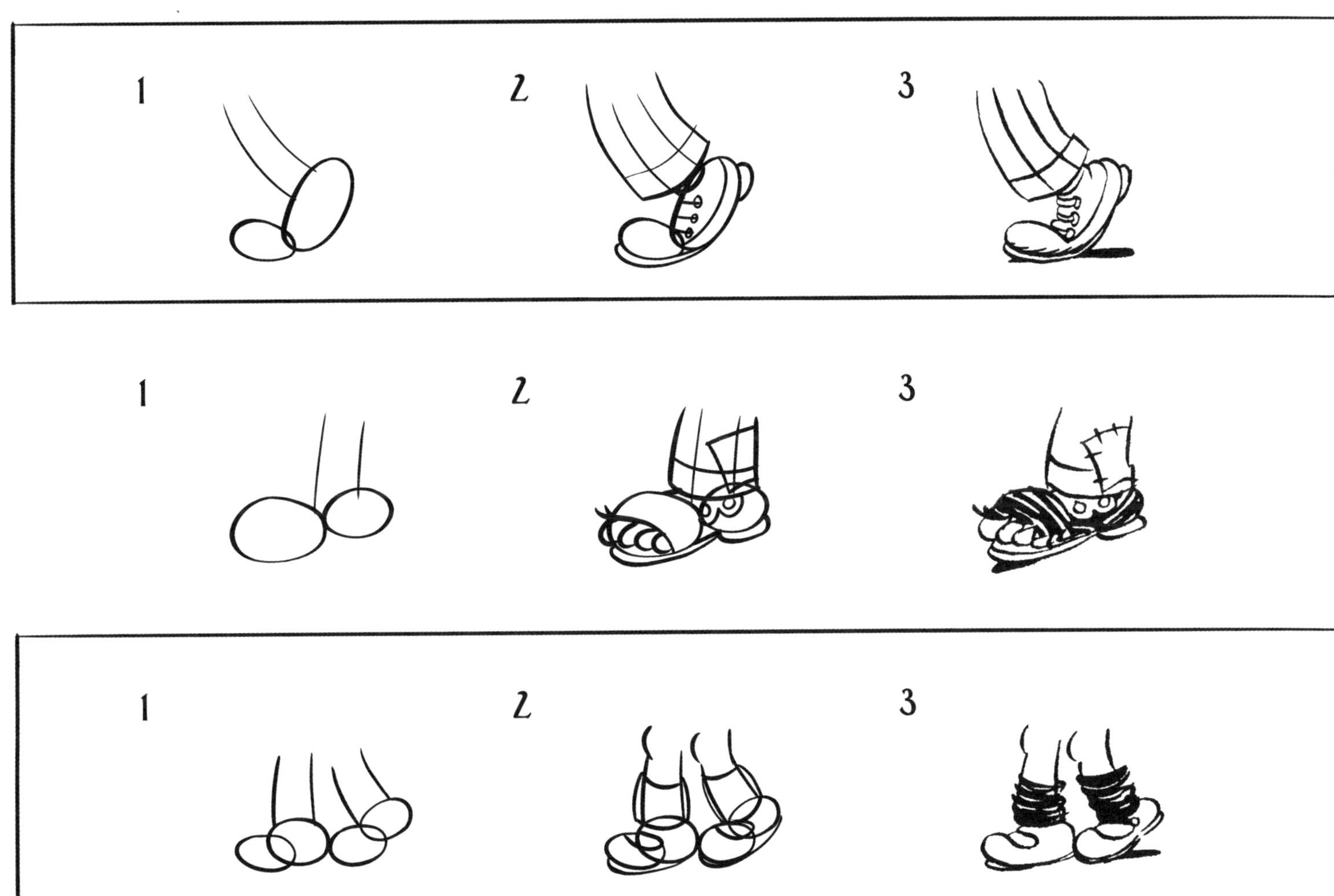
1
2
3
1
2
3
1
2
3

The Head

Start the simple comic head by making a rough circle in pencil, as shown on the opposite page. Next, divide the circle, as shown. Add the eyes, ears, nose, and mouth.

Study these pages and note how this is done. Notice the relative position of each feature to the others, and to the dotted lines. You'll see how the head looks in turning, then the same head expressing different emotions—surprise, sorrow, fright, deviousness, happiness, laughter, and anger. Study these drawings and you will see that the expression is changed, mainly, by altering the mouth, the eyes, and the eyebrows. Further on, you'll see the head tilted into various positions.

No doubt you will find this lesson more difficult than those prior to it, but stick to it and you will be surprised at your improvement. After you have studied the drawings, make a whole page of pencil circles and add the features as you conceive them, to express the various emotions. Then try turning the heads, and next, try drawing them in tilted positions.

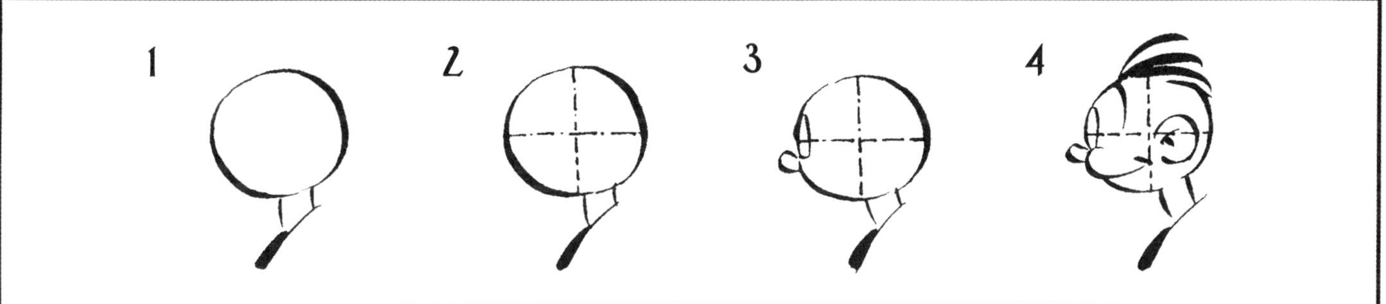

1
2
3
4

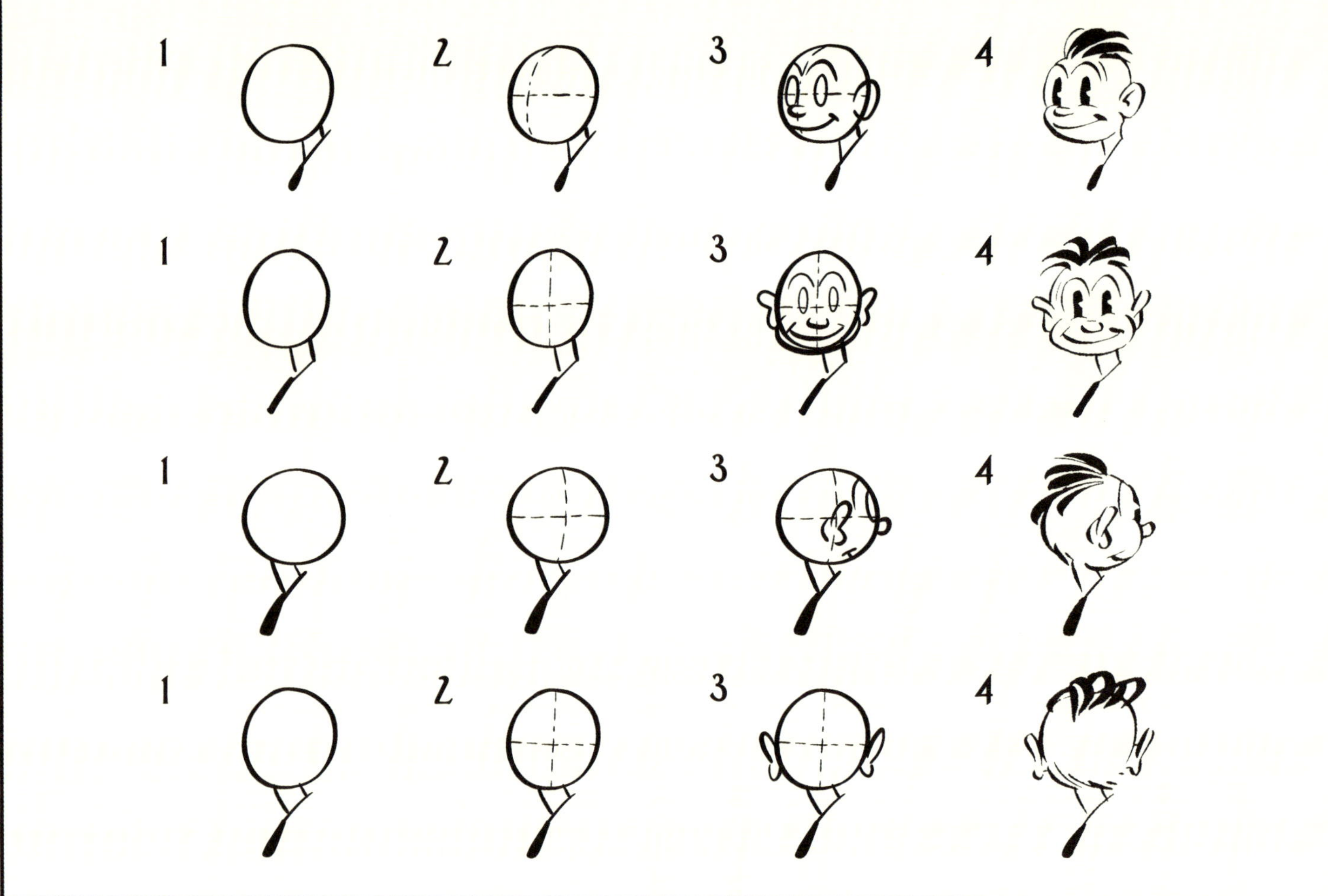

1
2
3
4
1
2
3
4
1
2
3
4
1
2
3
4

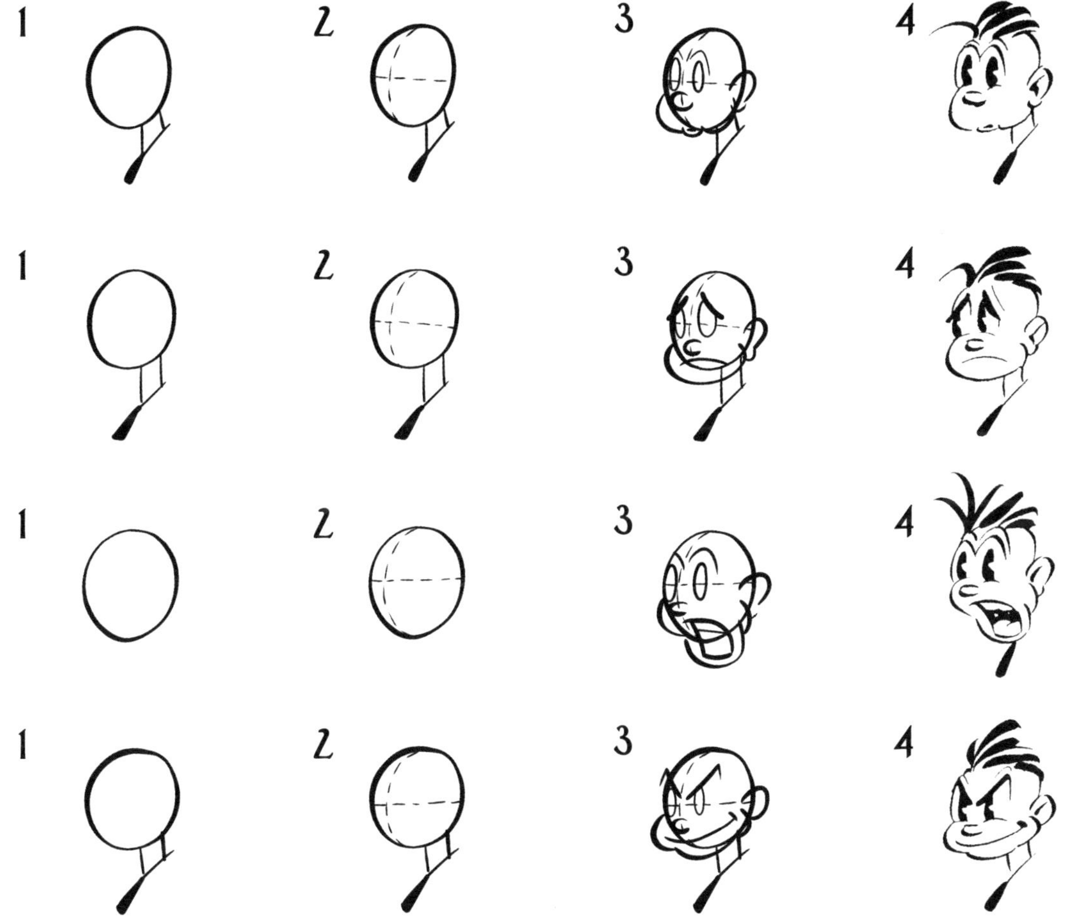

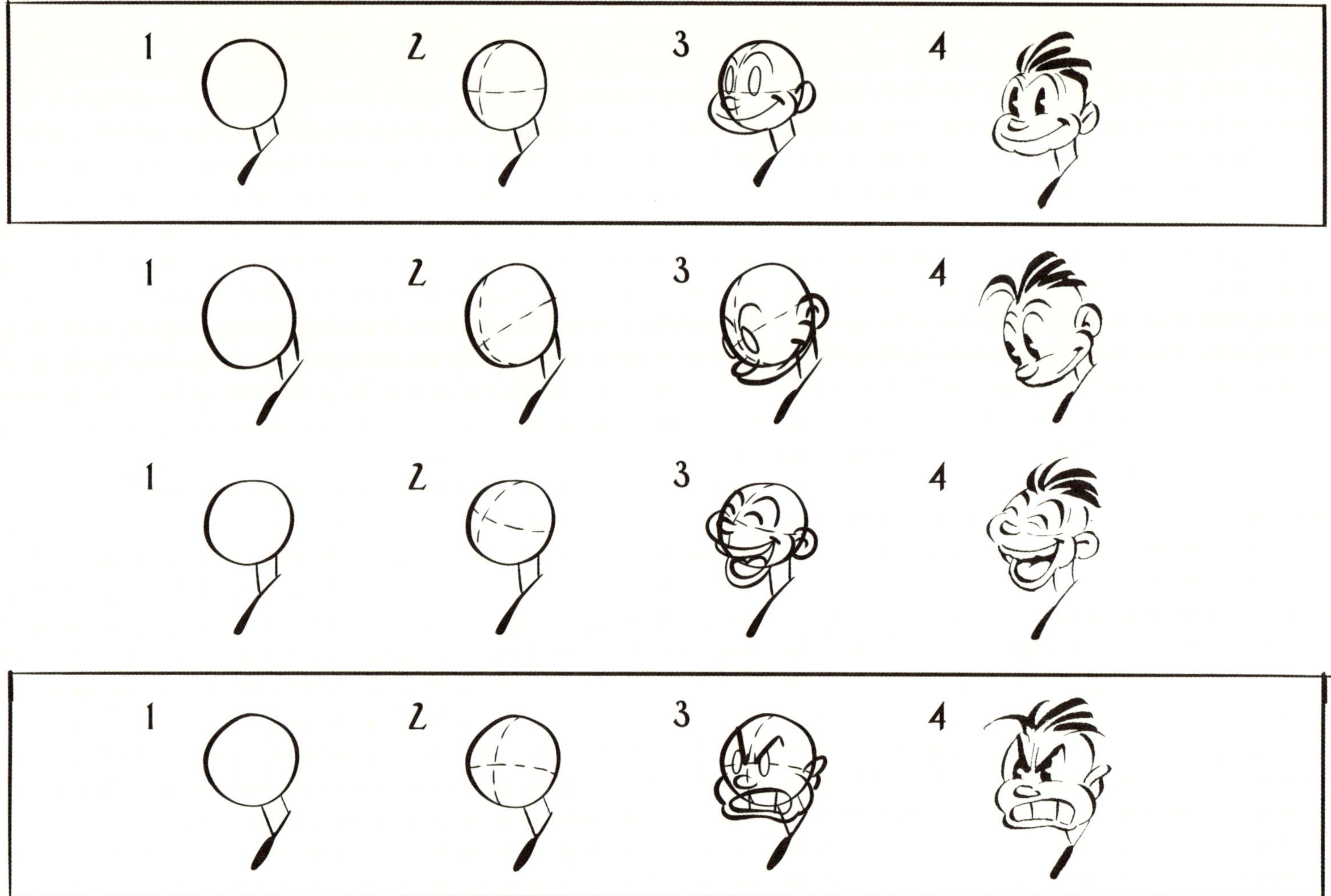

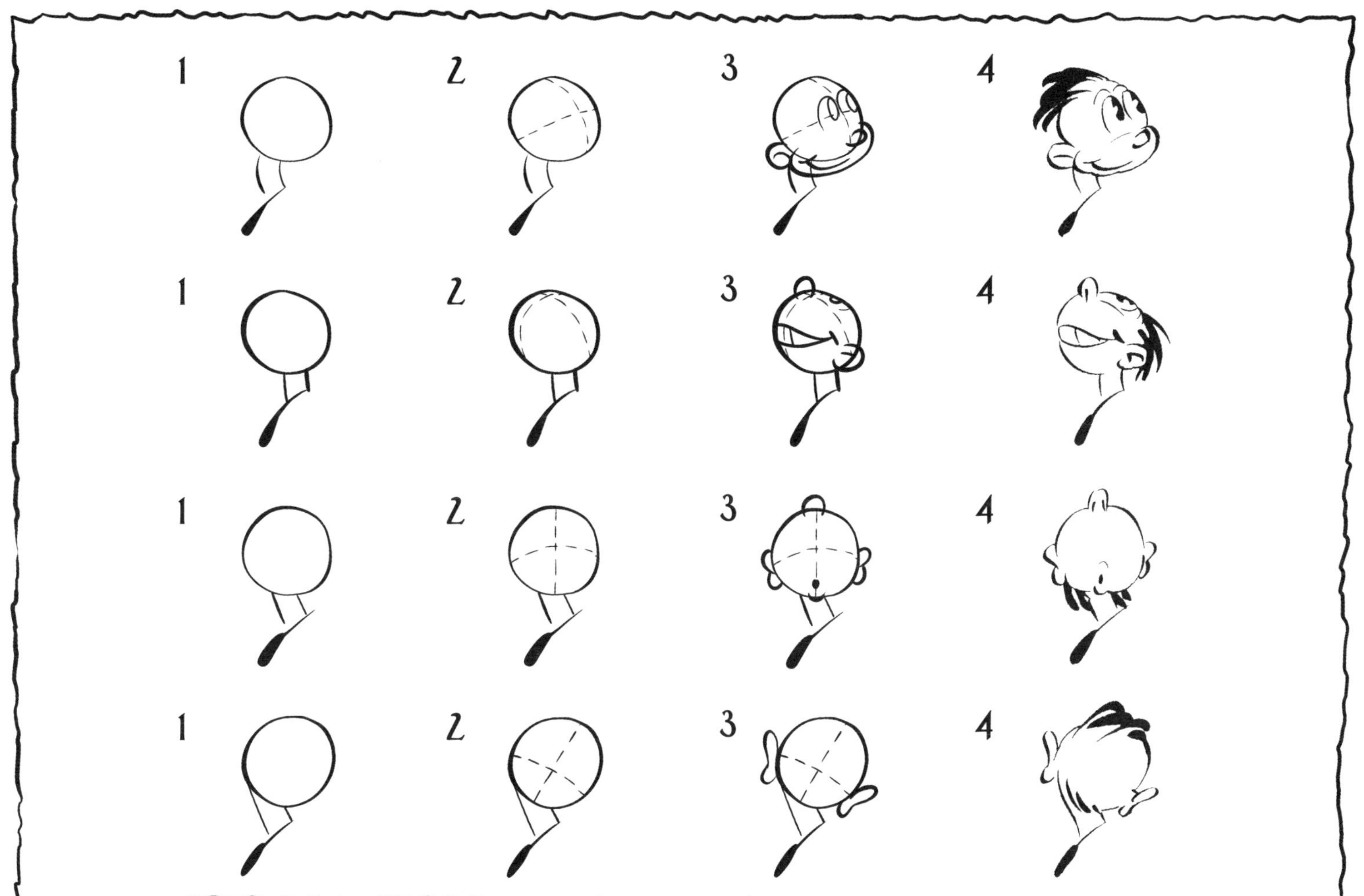

Character Heads

When you have become proficient at making heads from simple circles, you are ready to put character into your heads.

All types of heads cannot be suggested by a single circle, so we resort to a combination of circles to give us the framework for what might be called compound heads.

Note how the heads on the opposite page were first roughly penciled out, and then completed. The completed heads in this chapter were constructed originally on combinations of circles. Use them as examples and construct a page of heads from your own imagination.

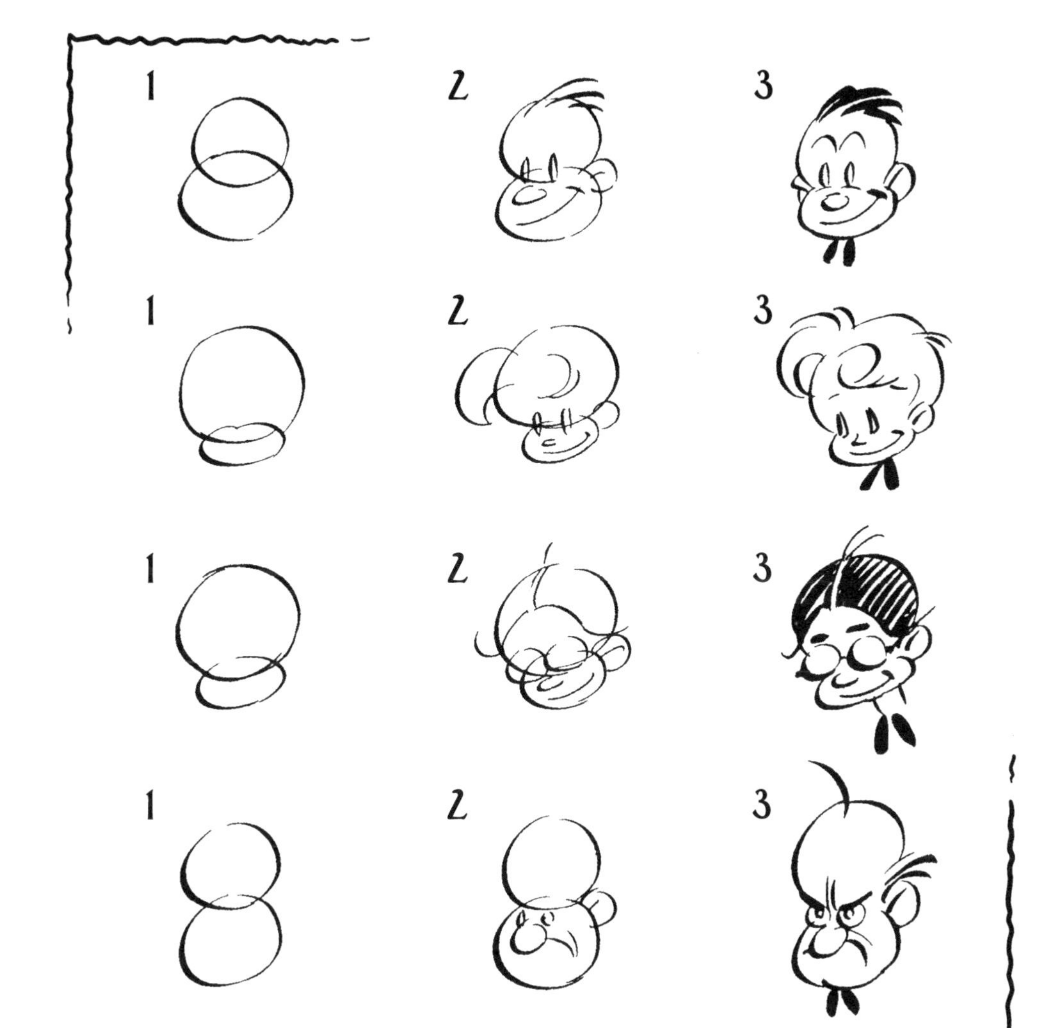

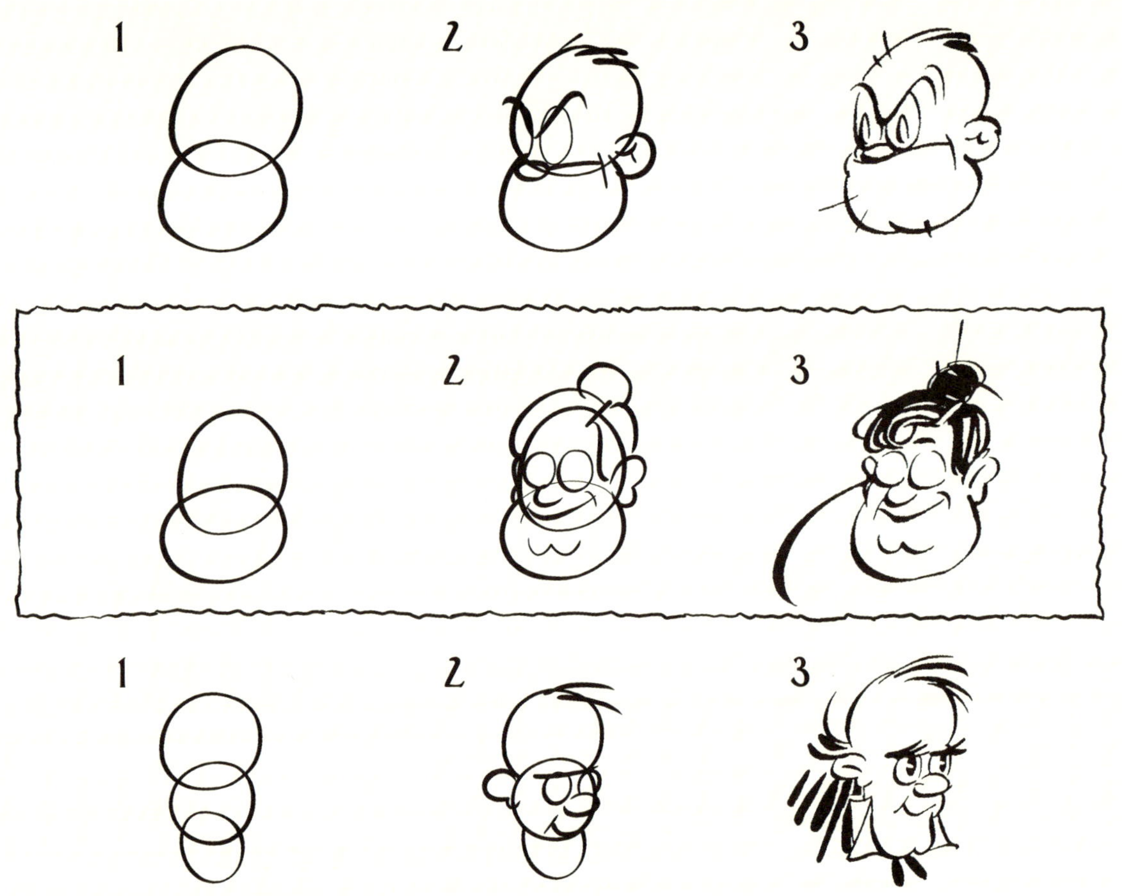

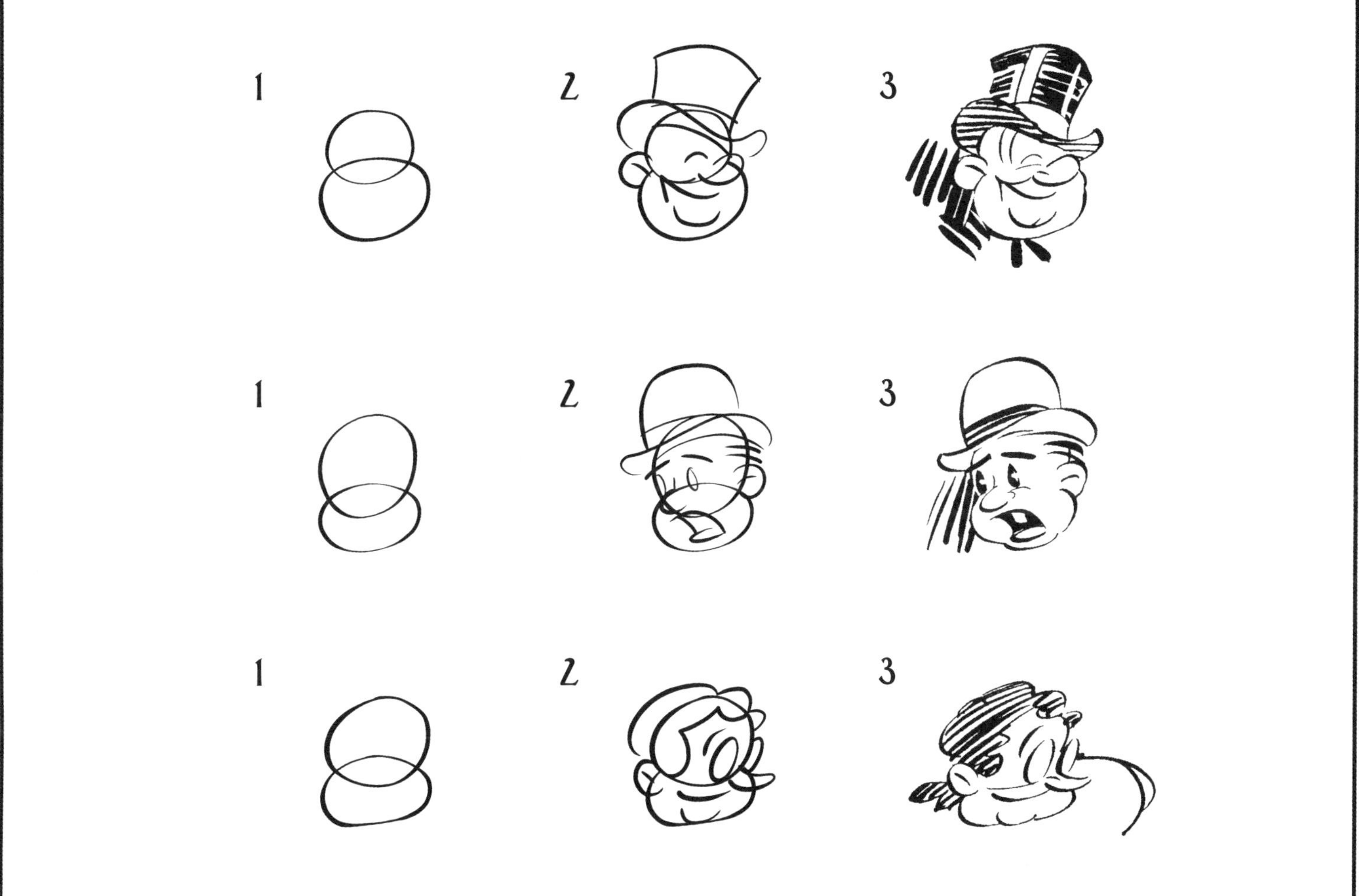

1
2
3
1
2
3
1
2
3

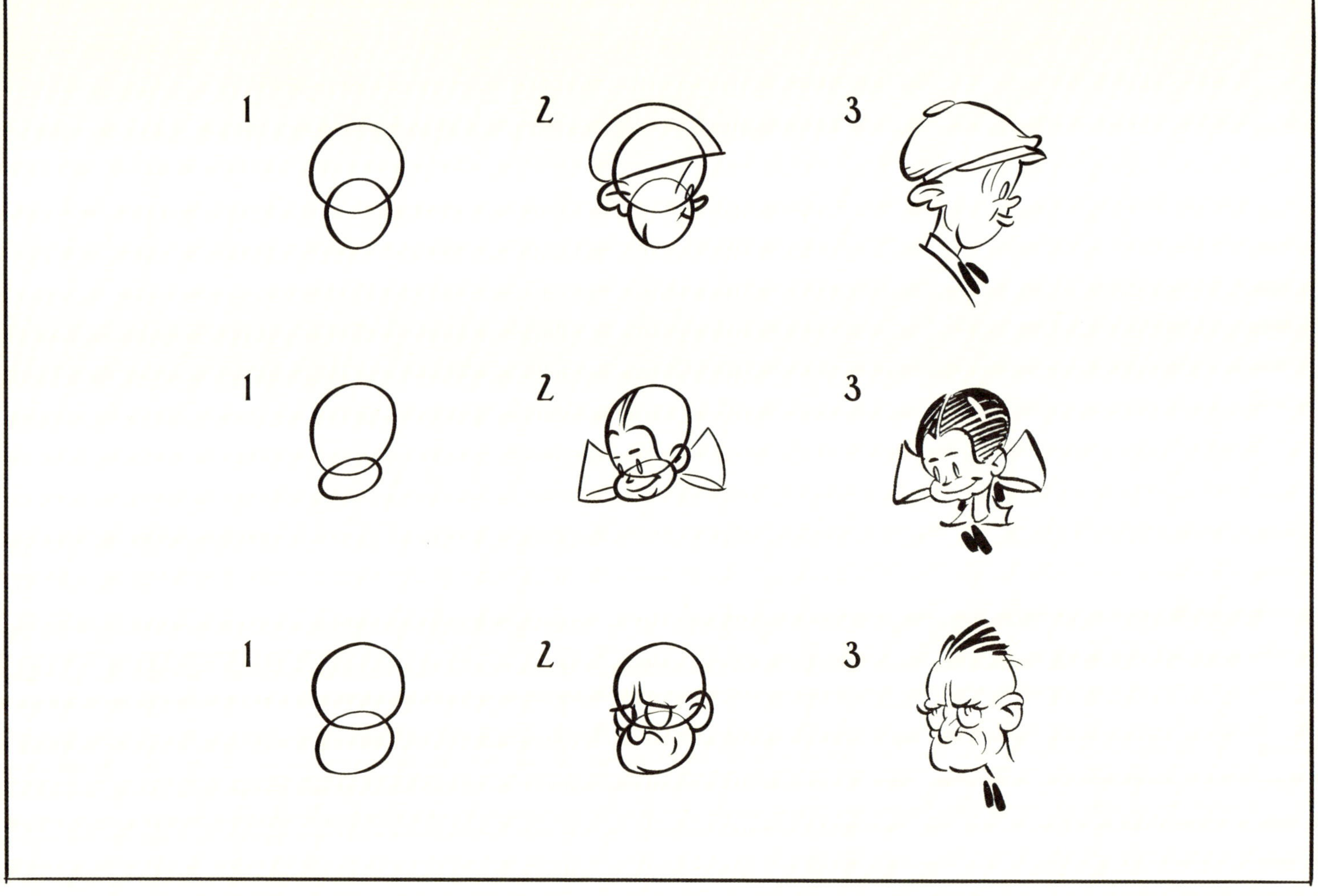

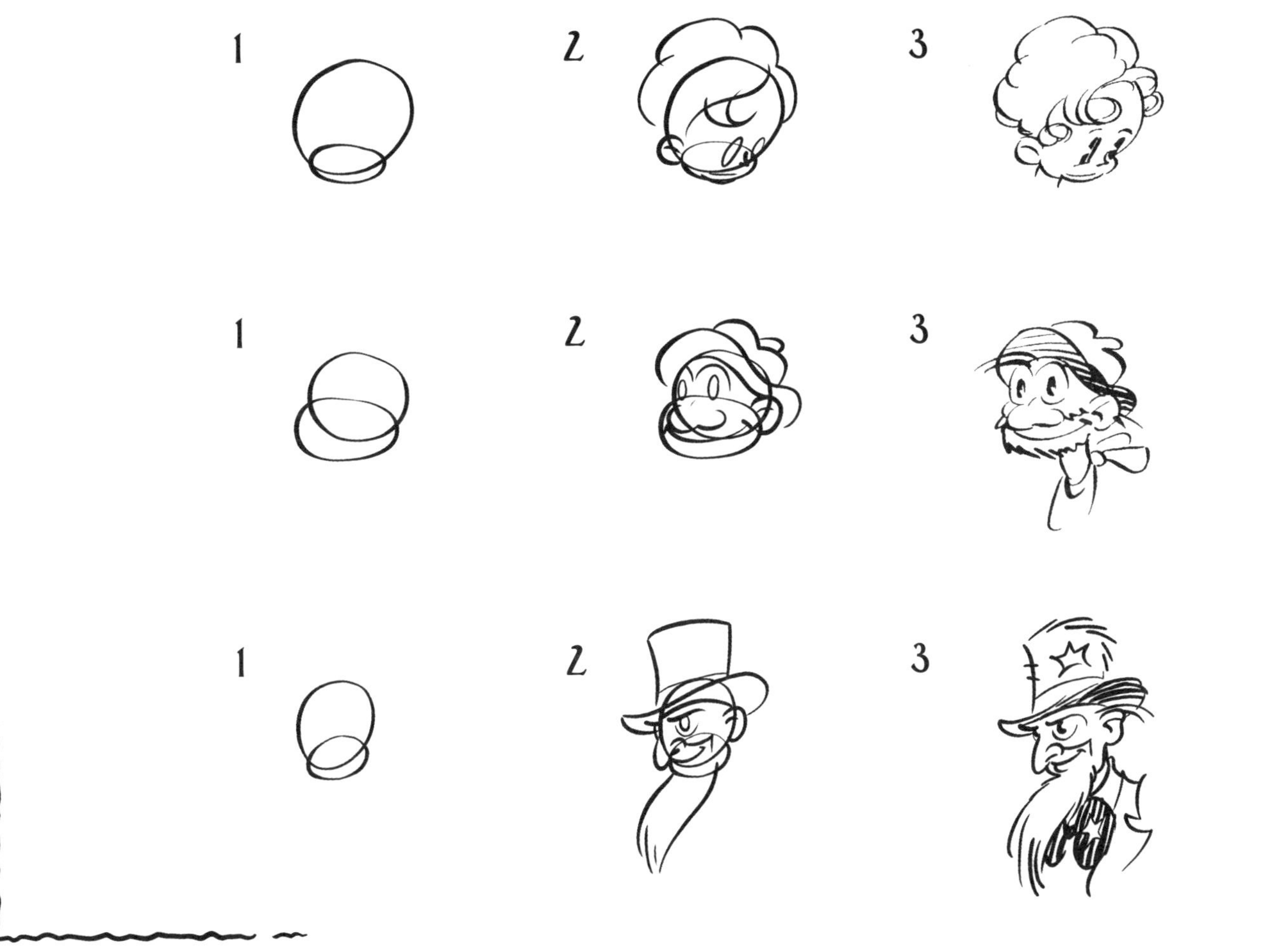

Comic Figures

The comic figure is first roughed out as a combination of circles. On the opposite page you will note that one circle is drawn to represent the head; another, the chest; and a third, the buttocks. Notice the relative positions of these circles, and also, see how the arms, legs, and feet are attached.

Practice making simple standing figures of your own. But, as figures would appear stiff if they were all drawn in erect positions, it is necessary to bend and foreshorten your figures to get action into your drawing. Note how this is done in the two figures over the page. The circles overlap one another, instead of being one above the other, as in the erect figure.

Try drawing figures in various attitudes, using these figures as your guide.

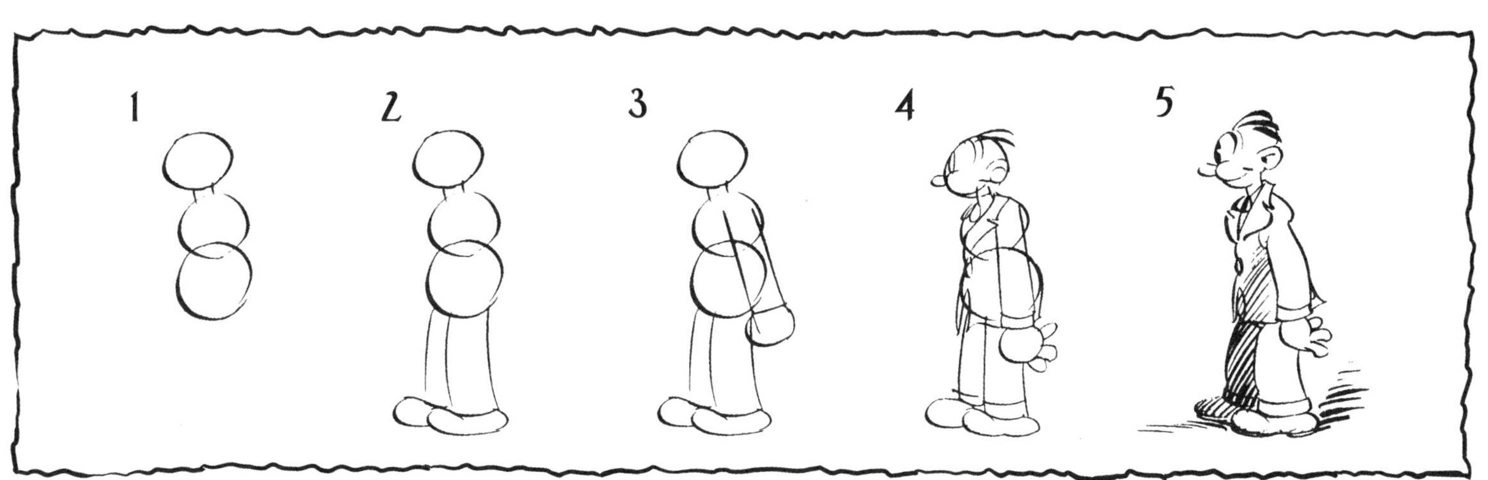

1
2
3
4
5

1   2   3

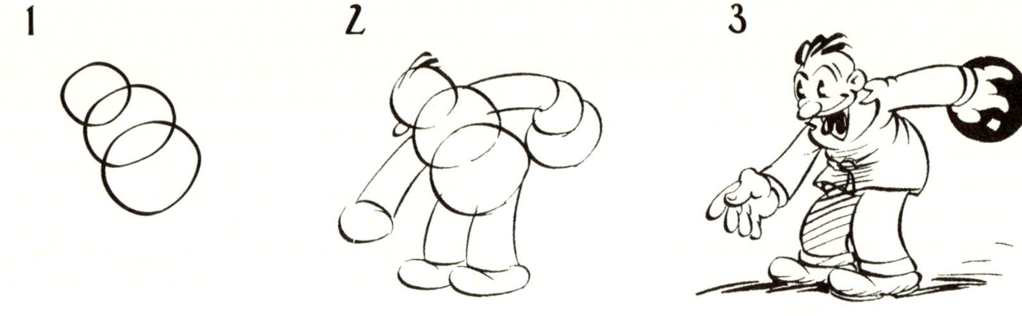

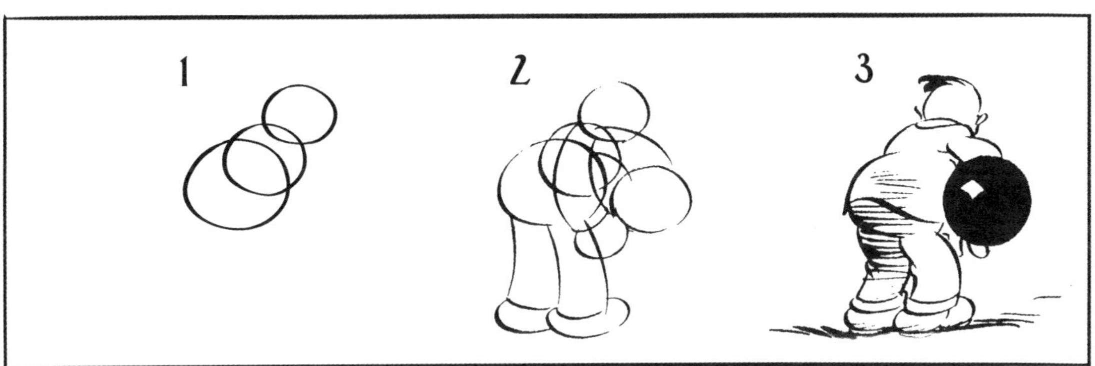
1
2
3

Action

This is really a continuation of the lesson on comic figures. The drawings on the opposite page were first roughed out, as detailed in the previous lesson, but the circles were arranged to make the figures more animated.

Comics are much more interesting if the characters seem to be doing something rather than remaining stationary. Rough out a page of figures in action, making them perform as ball players, golfers, divers, and runners. Use the examples as a guide at first, then make up a page from your own imagination.

You must eventually originate your own figures, so why not start early?

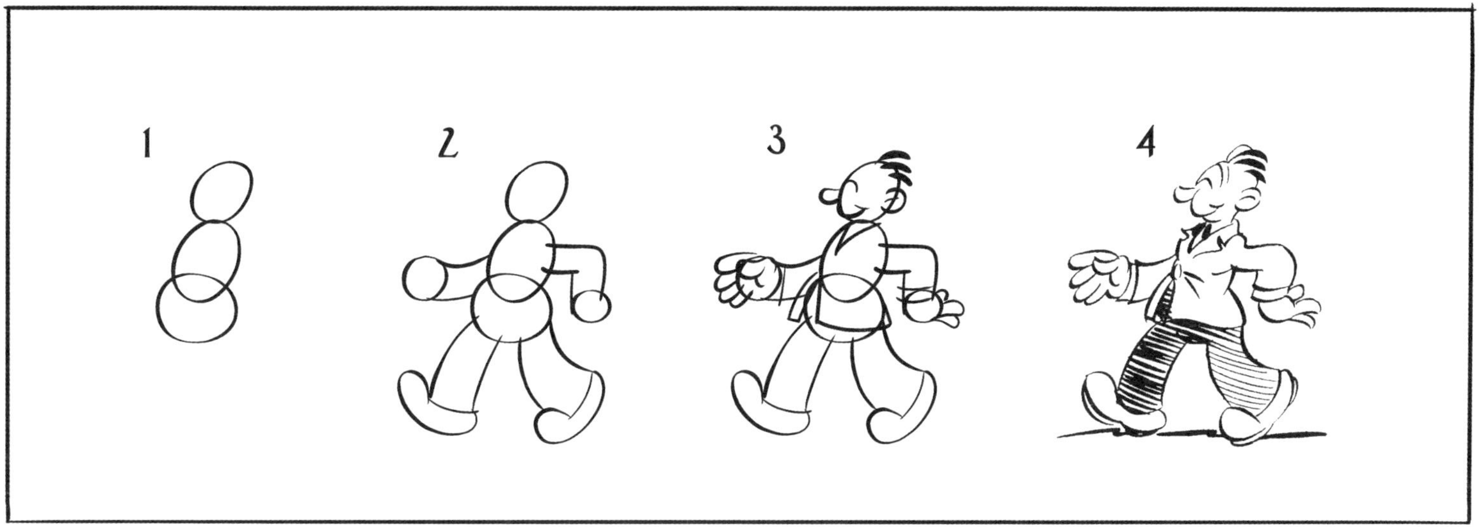

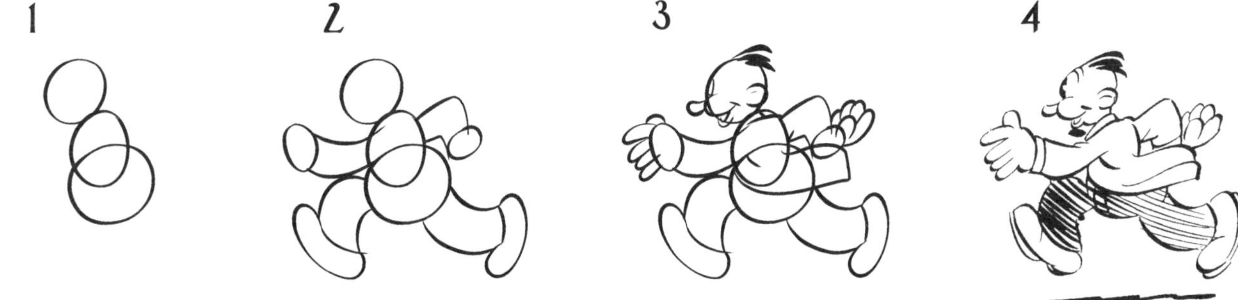

1
2
3
4
1
2
3
4

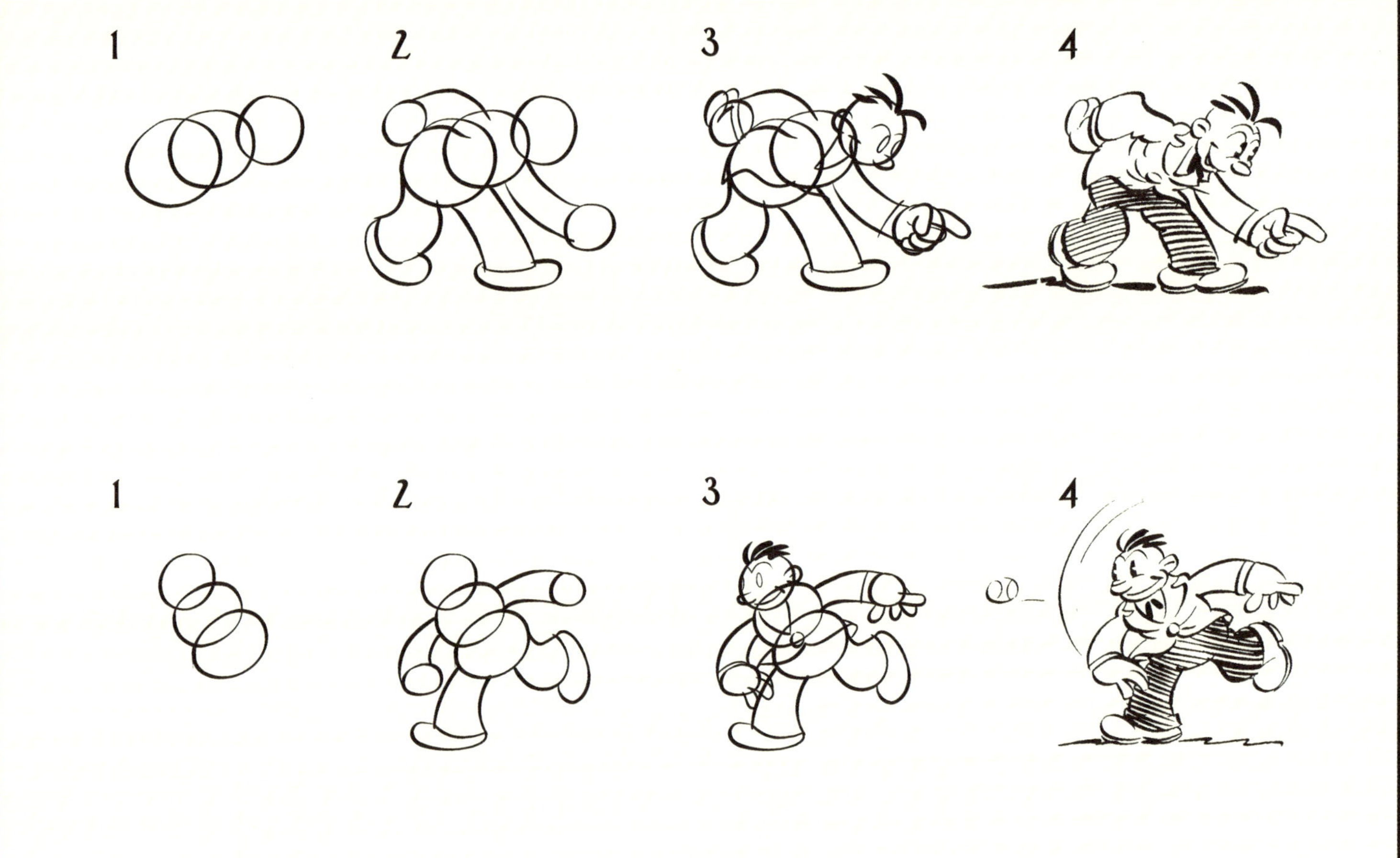
1
2
3
4
1
2
3
4

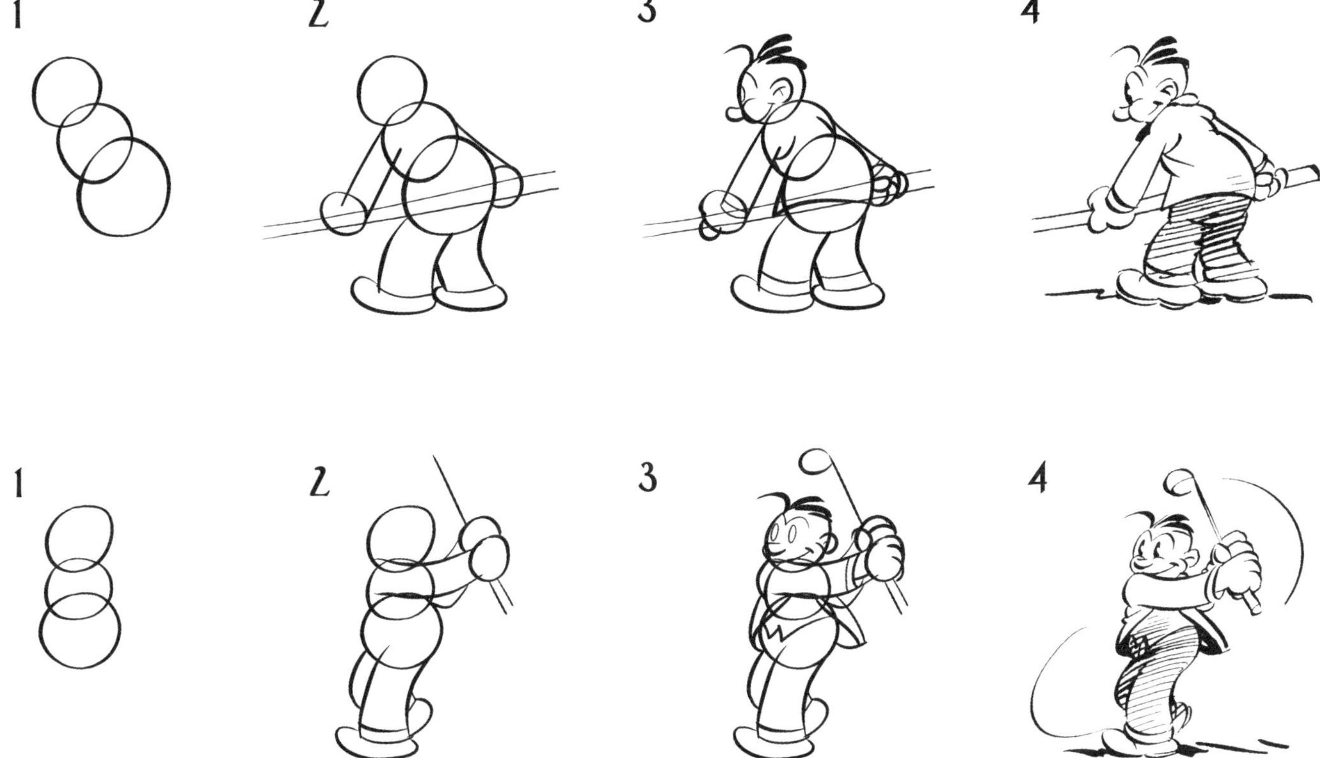

Comic Characters

Up to now, all the comic figures have been simple and built on the same combination of circles. Your work would look monotonous if every figure was alike, so we now advance to comic characters.

Character is achieved by varying the size of the circles. Note in this chapter the various combinations of circles used to construct the different figures. The policeman opposite is built by using a couple of large circles for the body. The chesty fellow on the following page was built by using a large upper circle and a small lower one. The little fellow opposite him has a small chest and large buttocks. The long-legged character after him, with the bundles, is still another combination.

Study these characters, and then make several pages of your own.

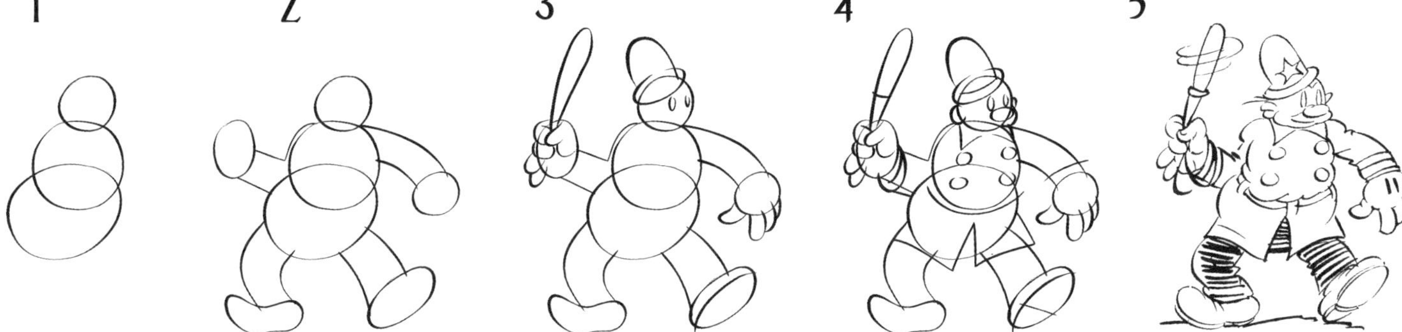

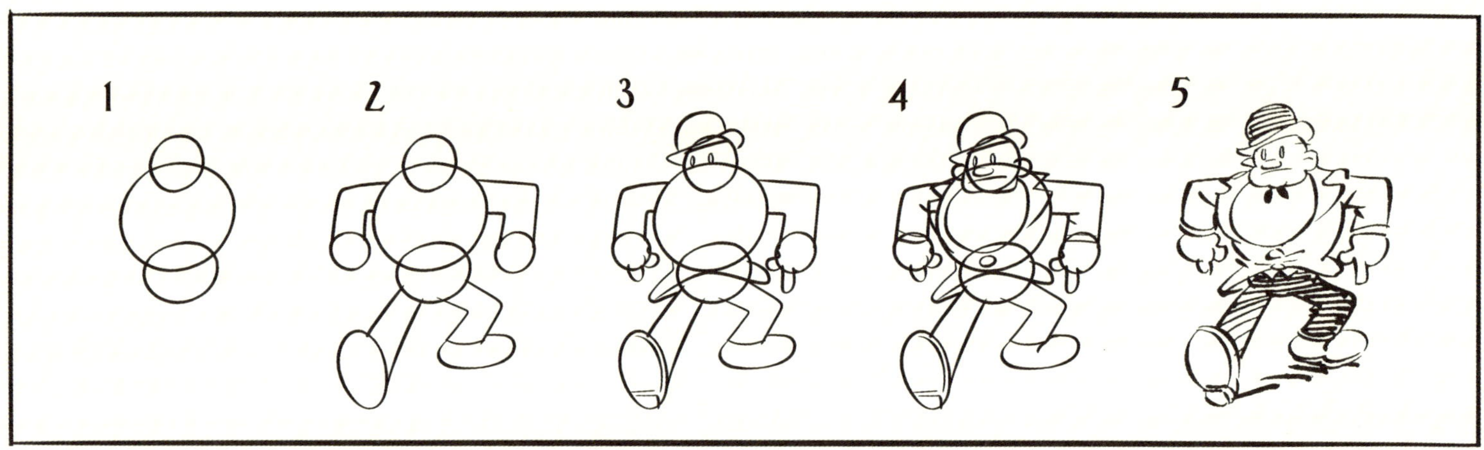
1
2
3
4
5

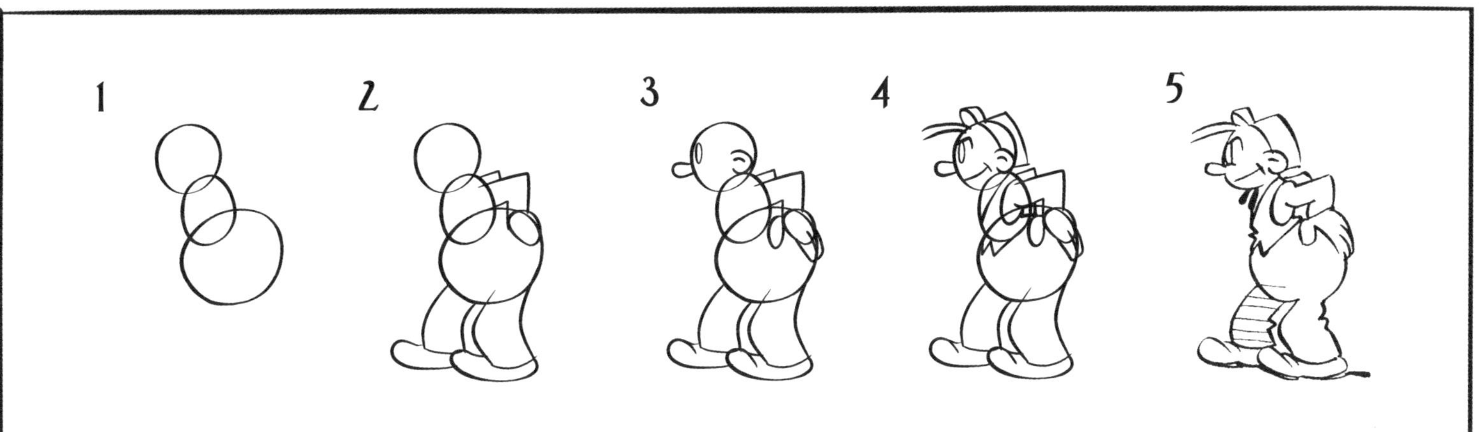

1
2
3
4
5

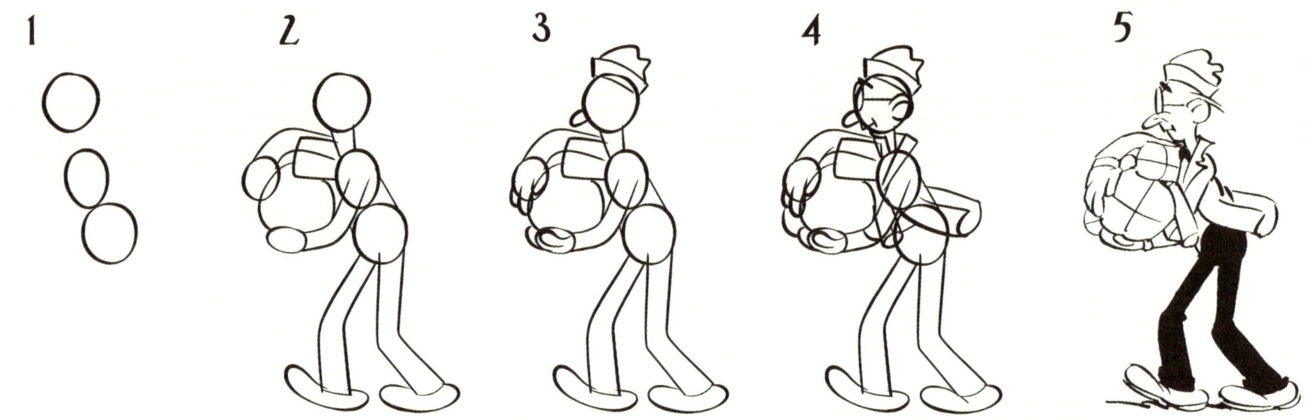

1
2
3
4
5

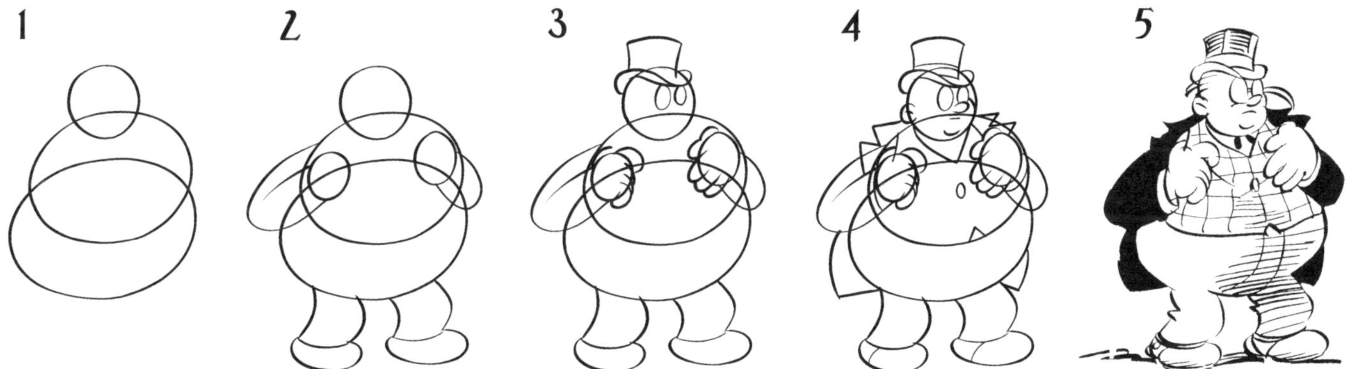

1
2
3
4
5

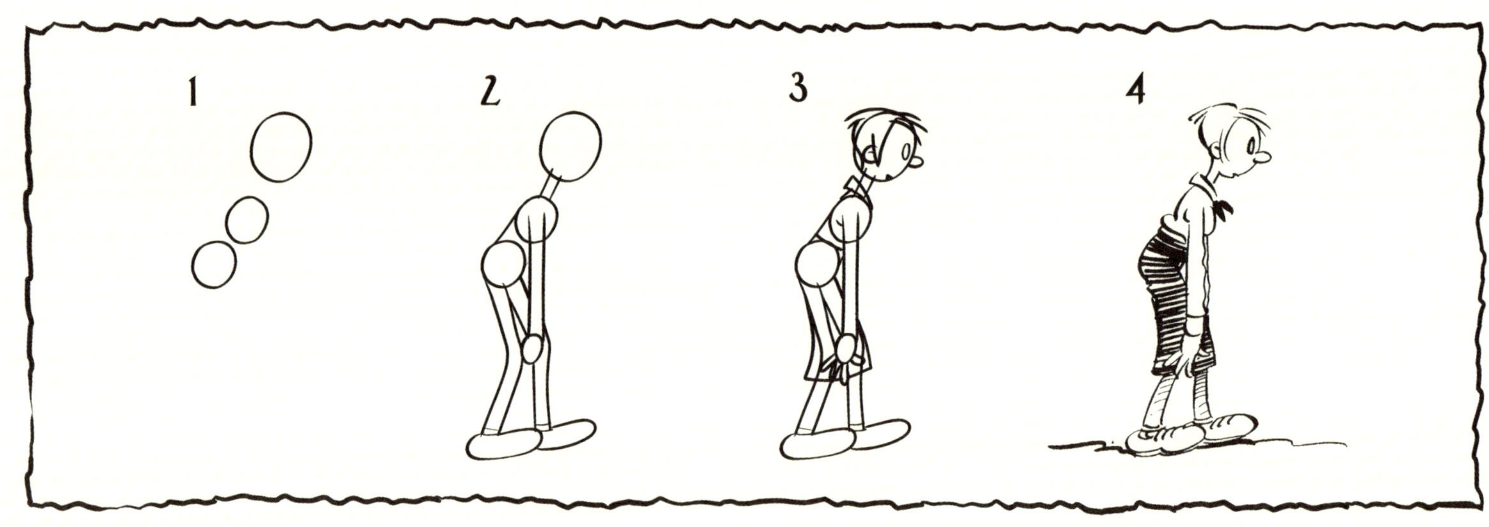

1   2   3   4

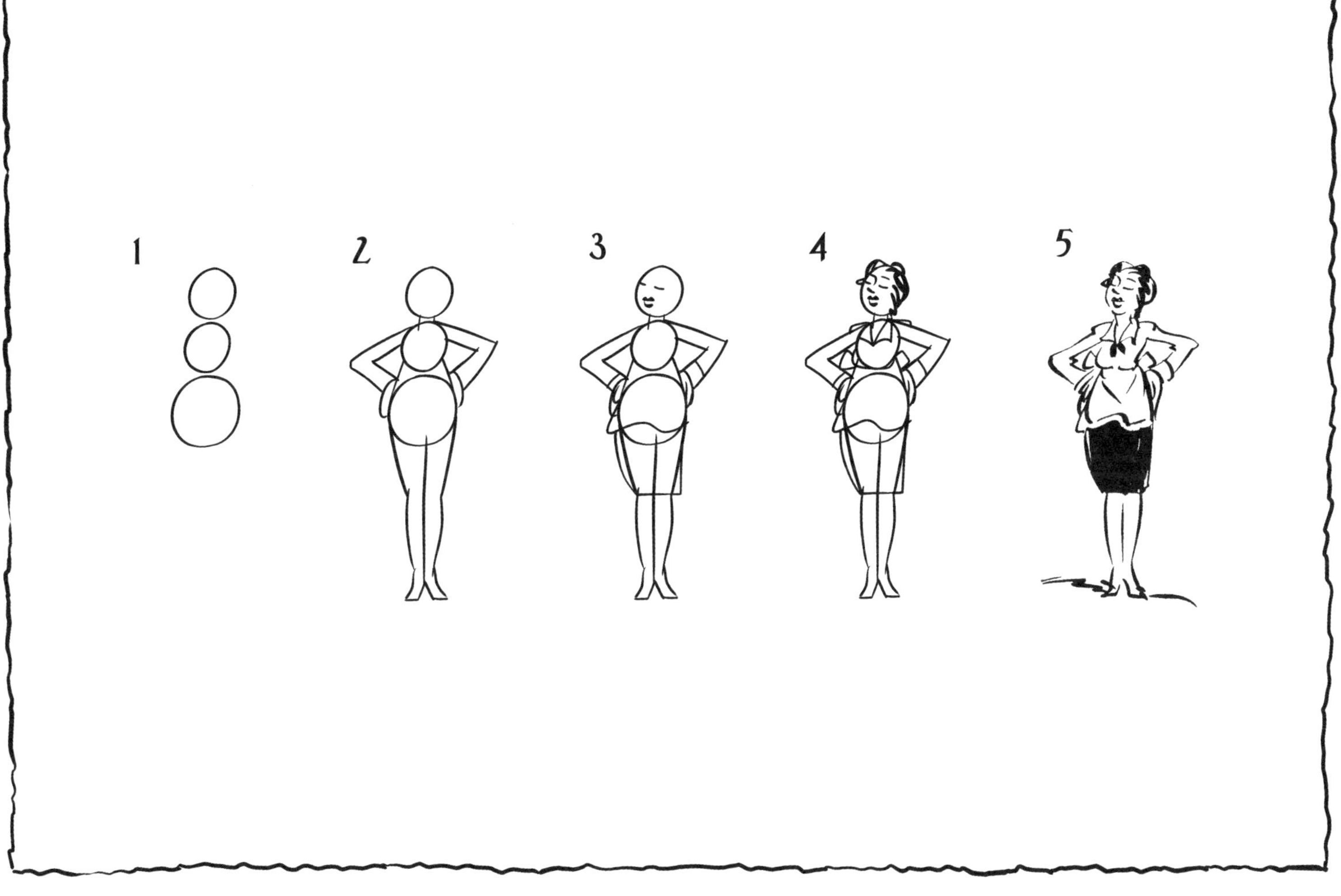

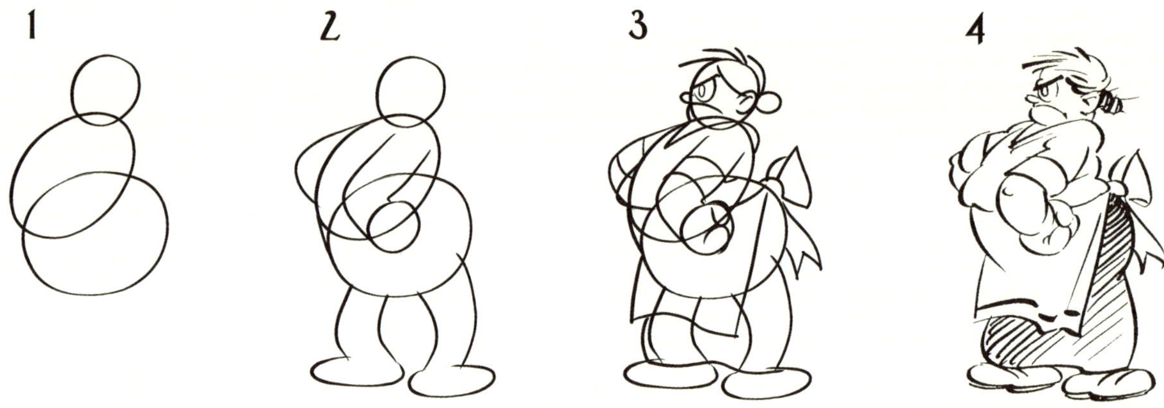

1
2
3
4

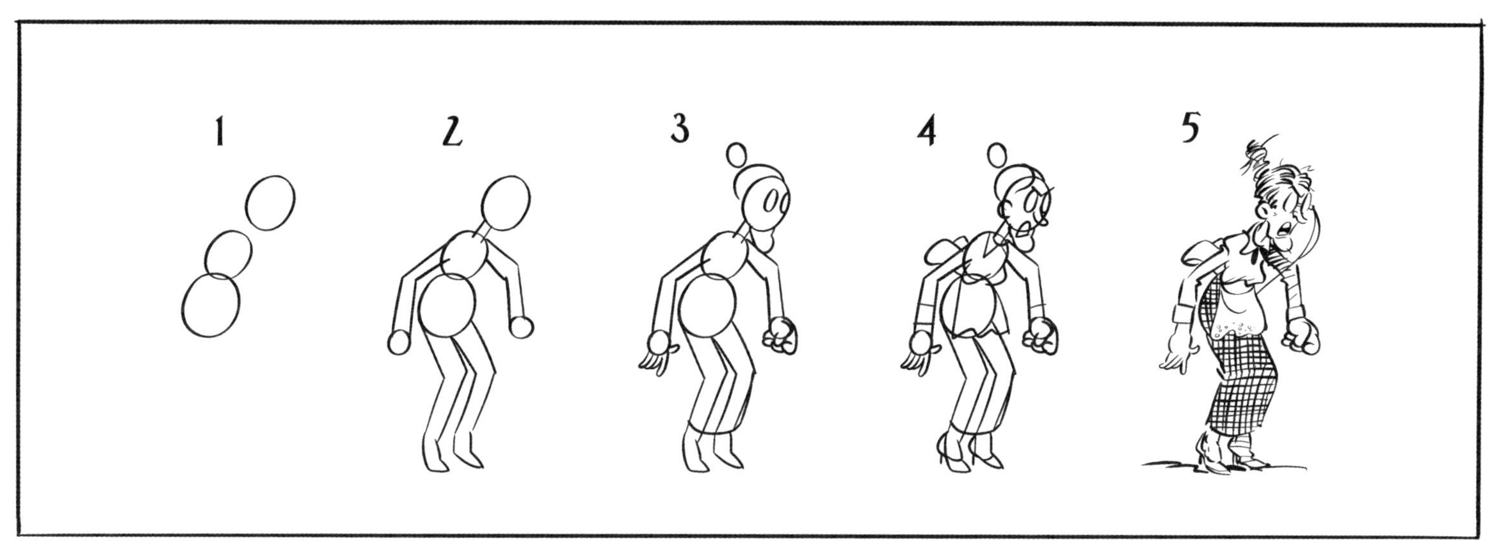
1
2
3
4
5

Children

Children are the comic artist's chief stock-in-trade.

There are two points to particularly note in the drawing of children. One is that it is better to use two circles to make the head; the upper circle always being the larger. The other point is that the head is large in relation to the size of the body. On the opposite page, these points are brought out graphically.

Study the drawings in this lesson and then make several pages of your own conception of children. Use the knowledge that you have gained from the preceding lessons to make your "action" poses. Draw them running, jumping, playing marbles, and acting as children do.

Children are seldom still, and if you draw them just standing, they will not look natural.

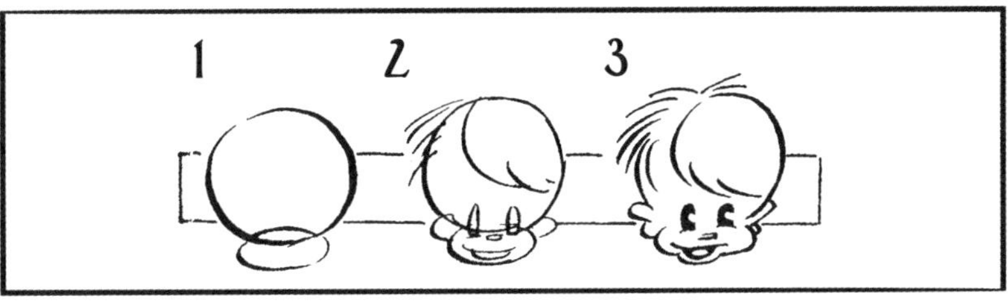

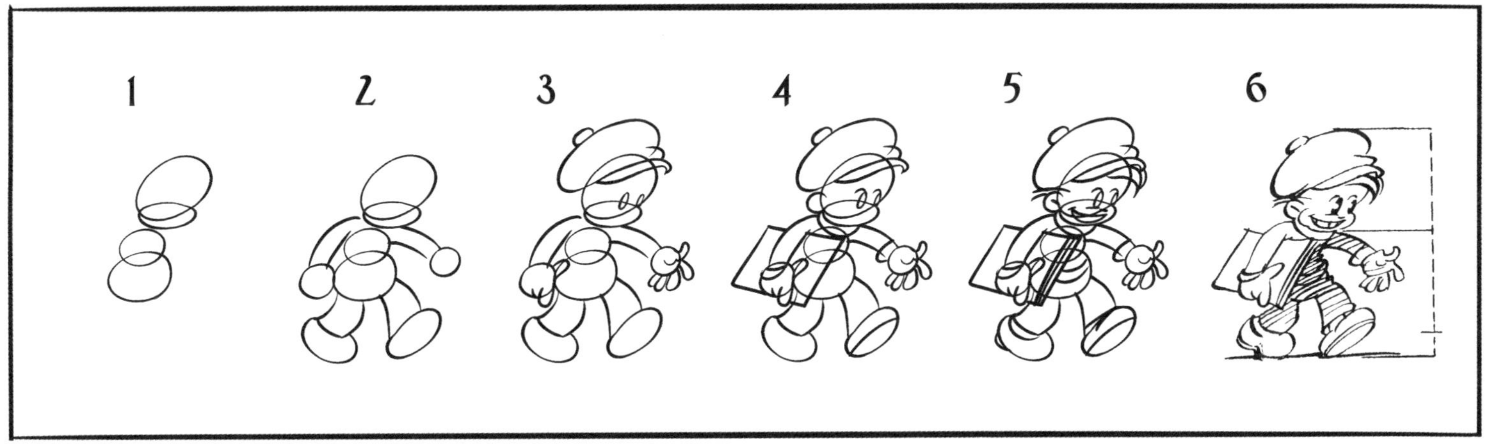

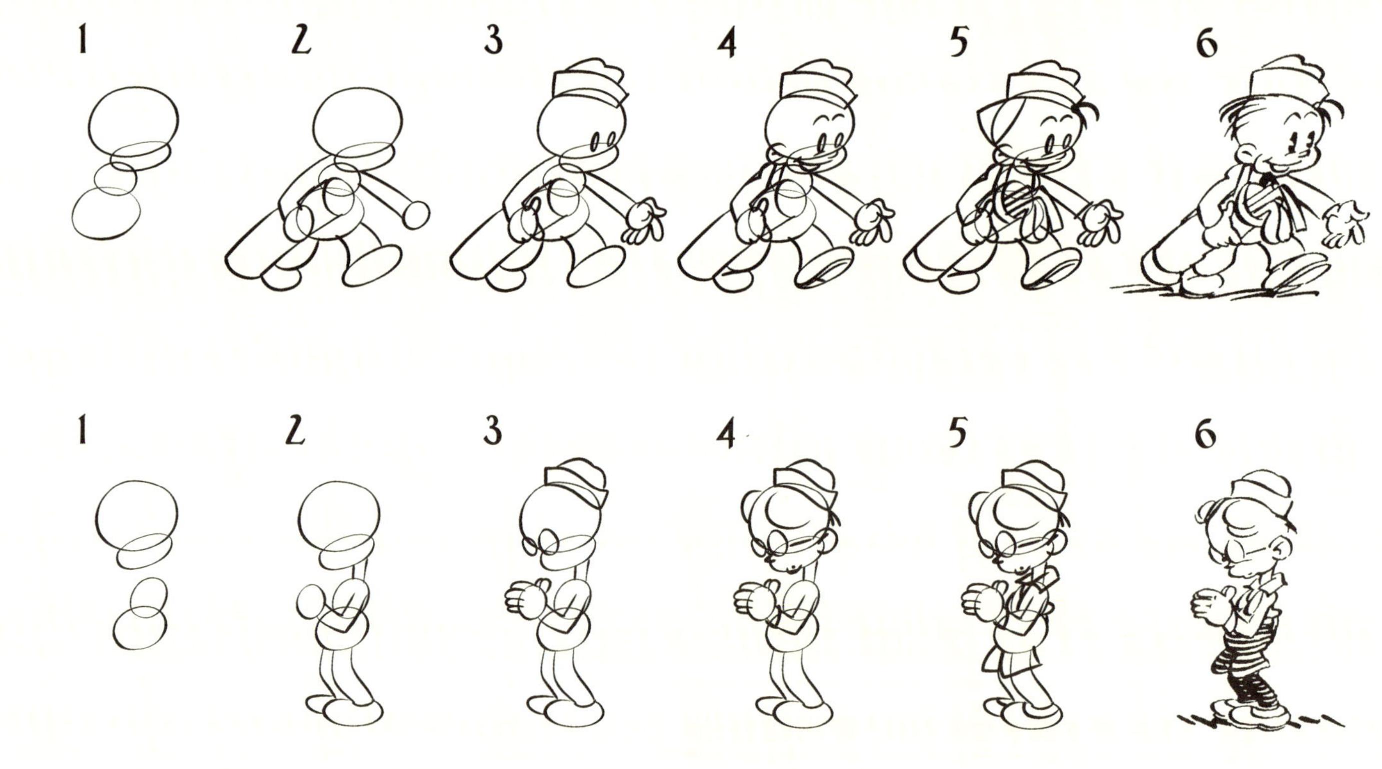
1
2
3
4
5
6
1
2
3
4
5
6

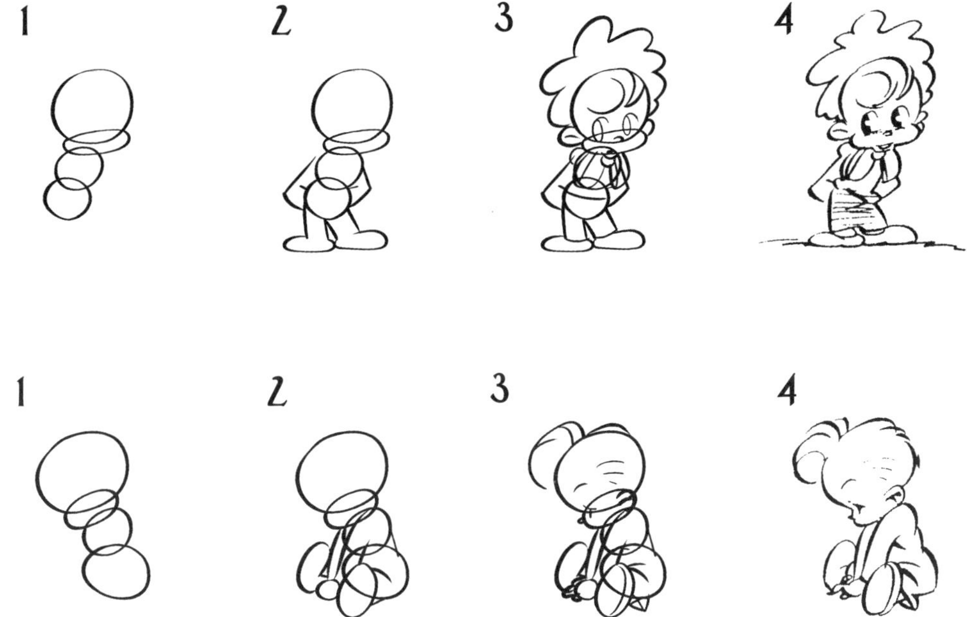

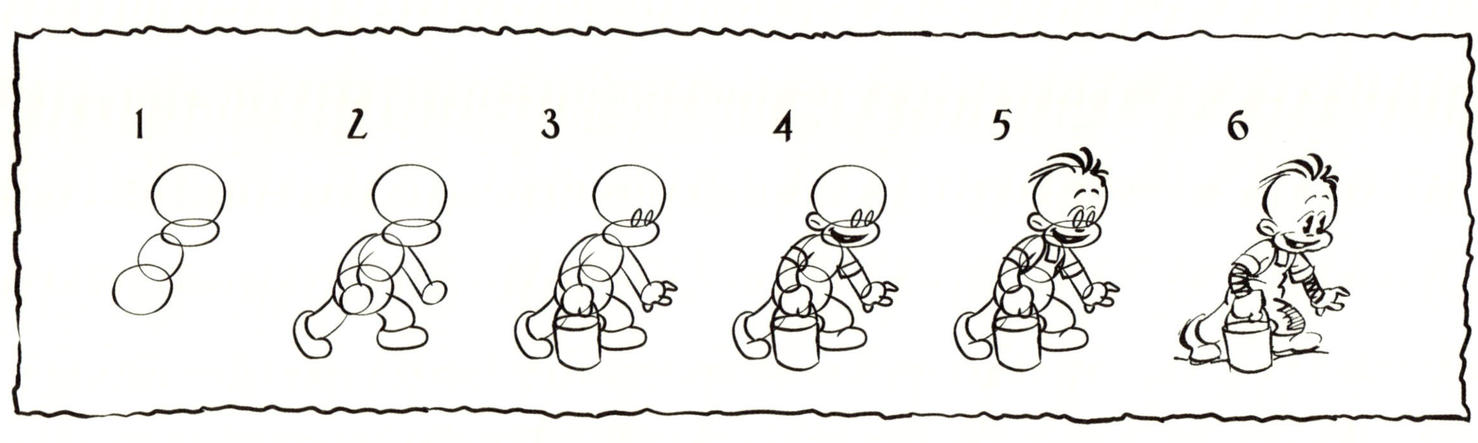

1
2
3
4
5
6

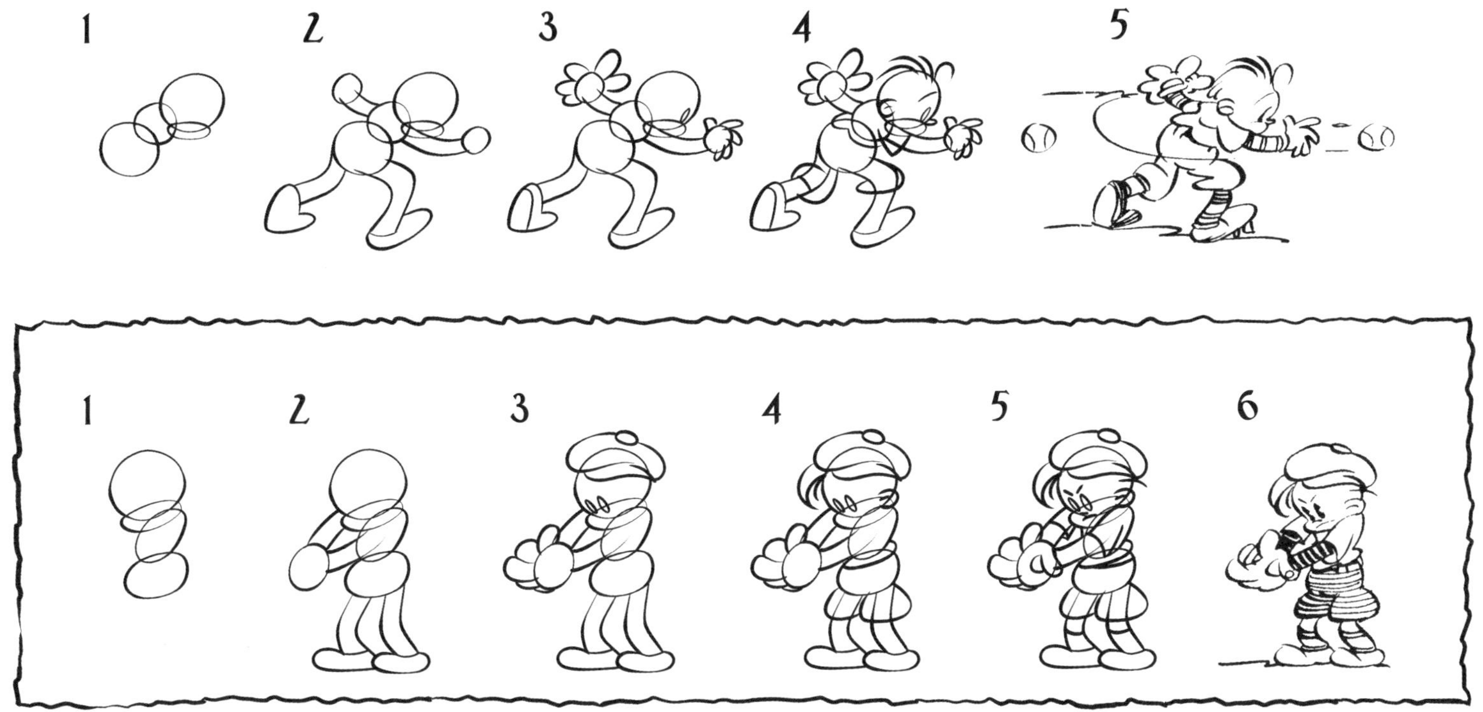

1
2
3
4
5
1
2
3
4
5
6

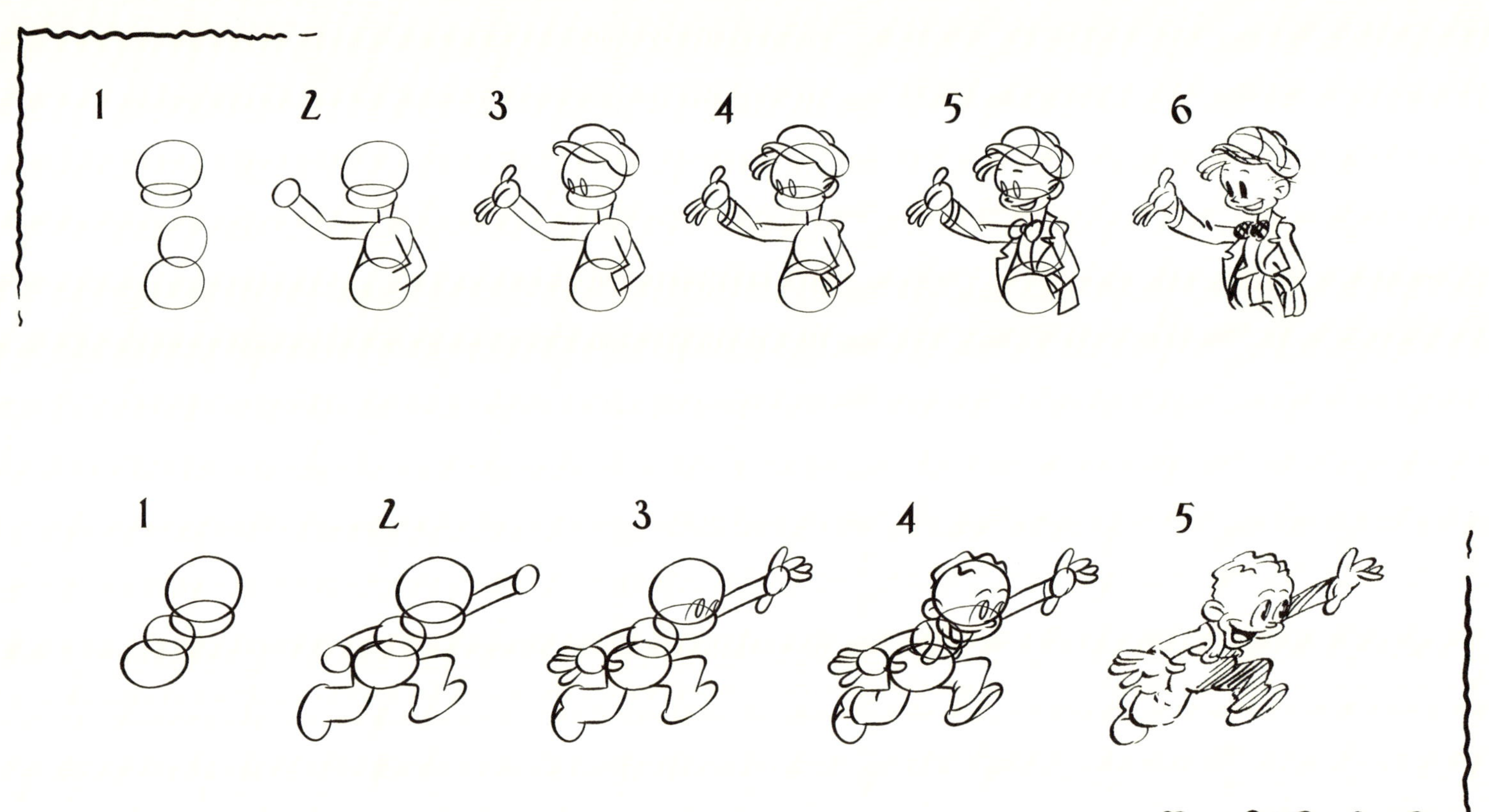
1
2
3
4
5
6
1
2
3
4
5

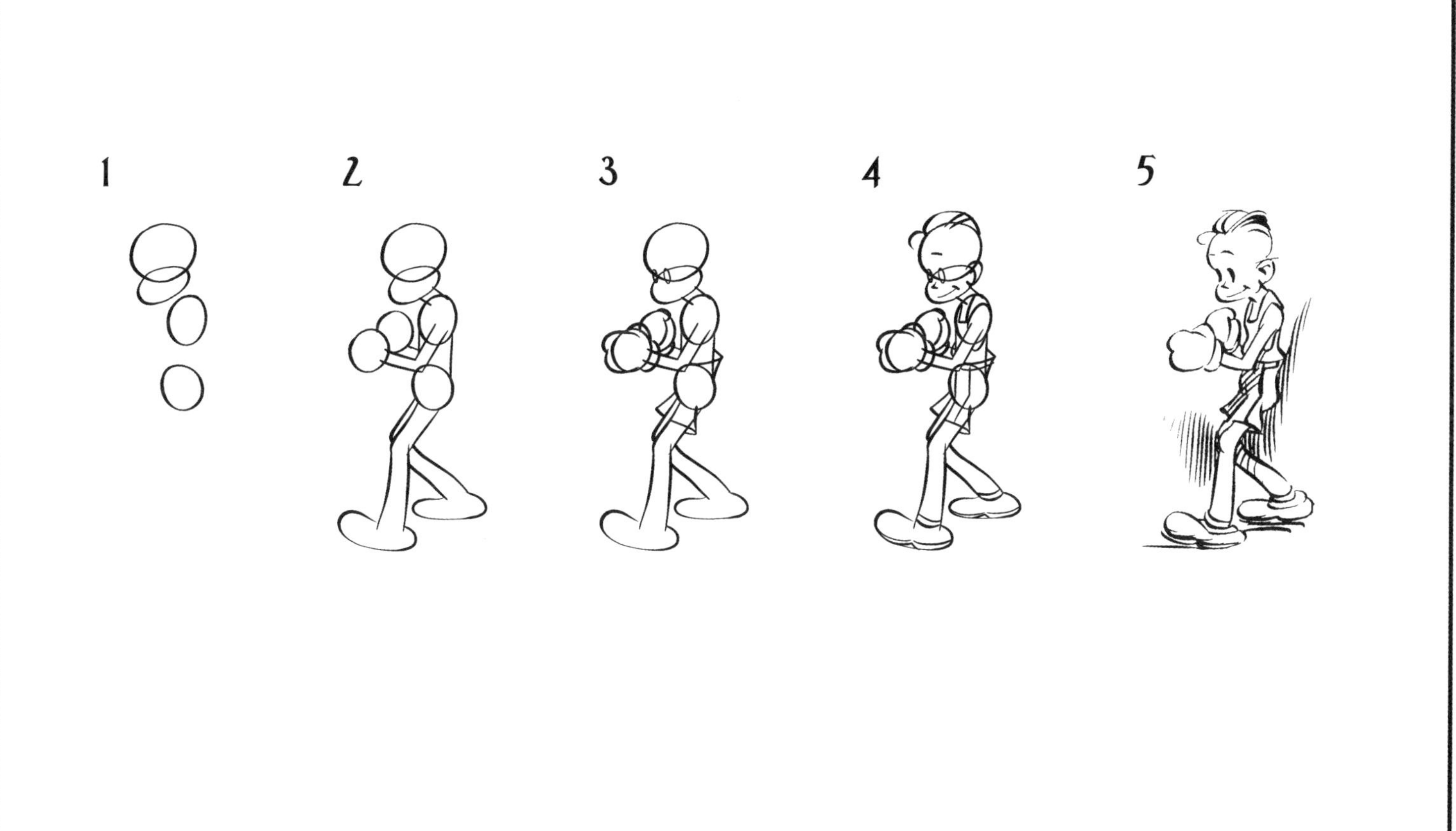
1
2
3
4
5

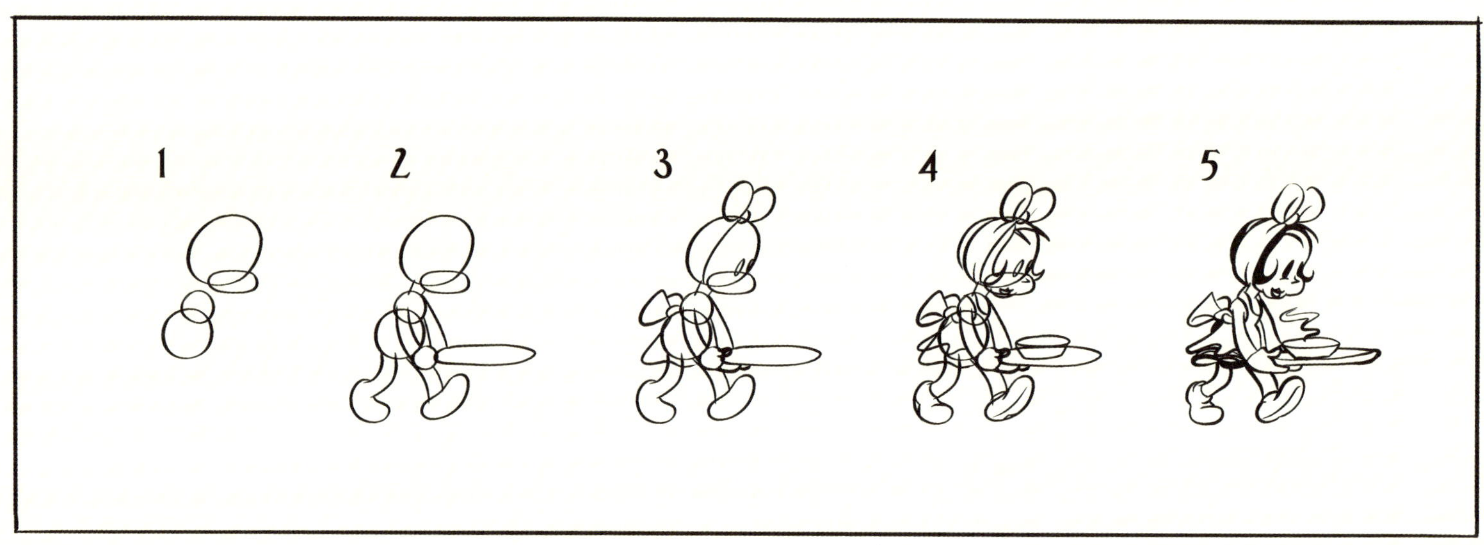

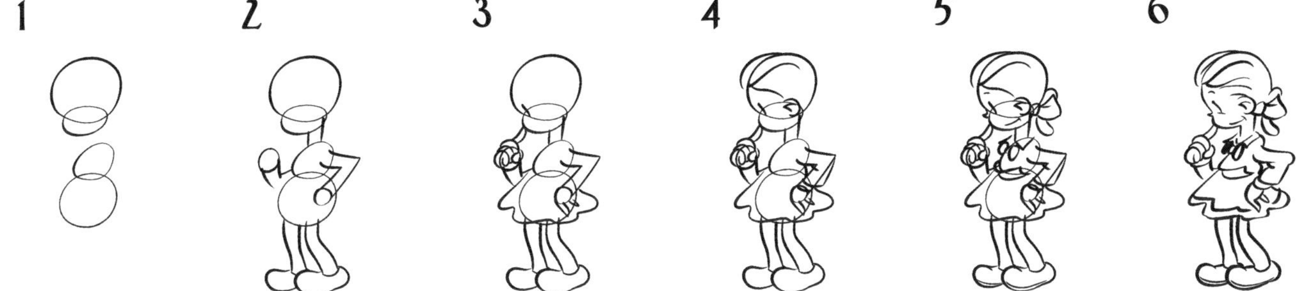

1
2
3
4
5
6

Animals

Comic animals are constructed with a circle understructure just as human figures are. Notice on the next few pages how the cat, dog, and horse were first roughed out and then finished. Notice that the cat is walking like a human being. This doesn't happen in real life, but in drawing comics you can take many liberties.

In this lesson you will find a variety of comic animals. Study them, for they are all made from combinations of circles. Try a few pages of animals, using the same characters as are drawn here, but put them in different positions. Make the dog run instead of walk; draw the cat jumping; and make the horse walk as the dog is walking.

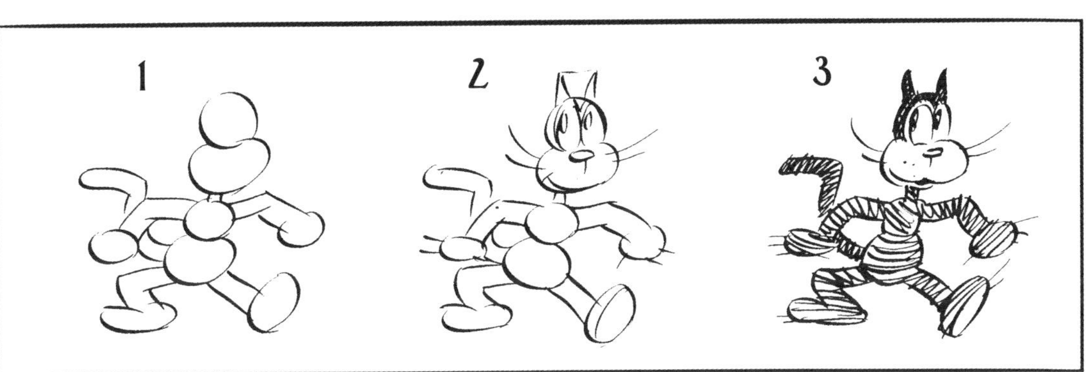
1
2
3

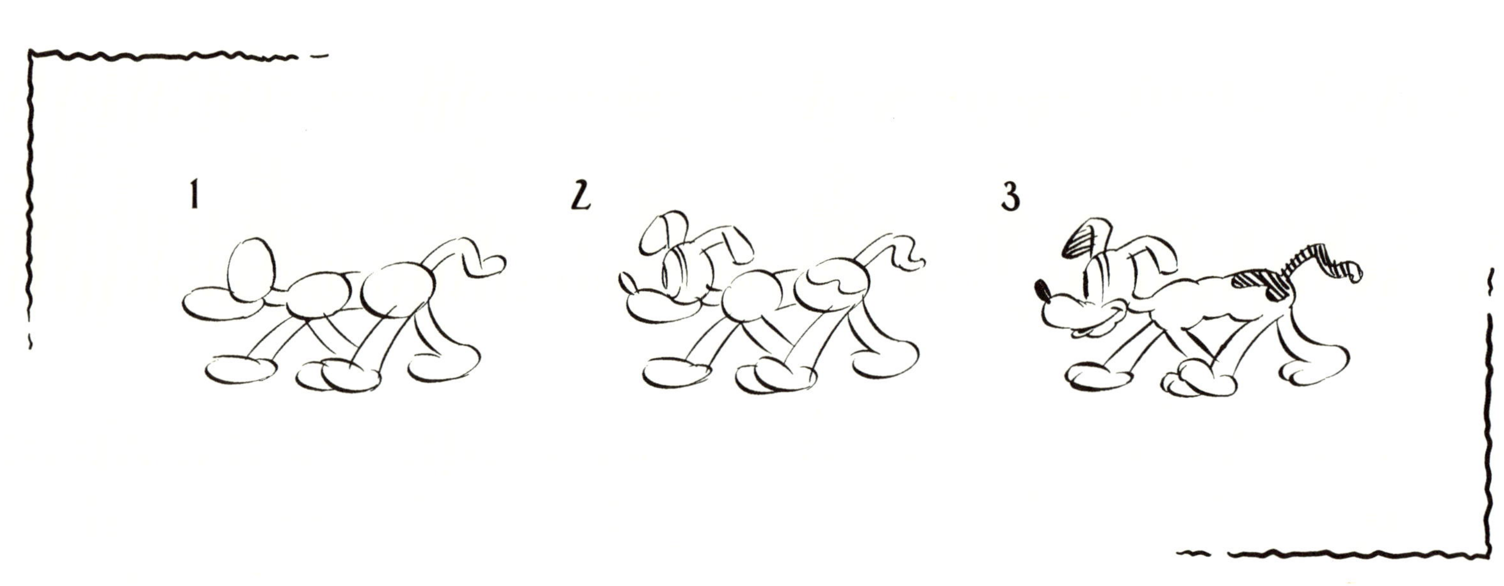
1
2
3

1 2

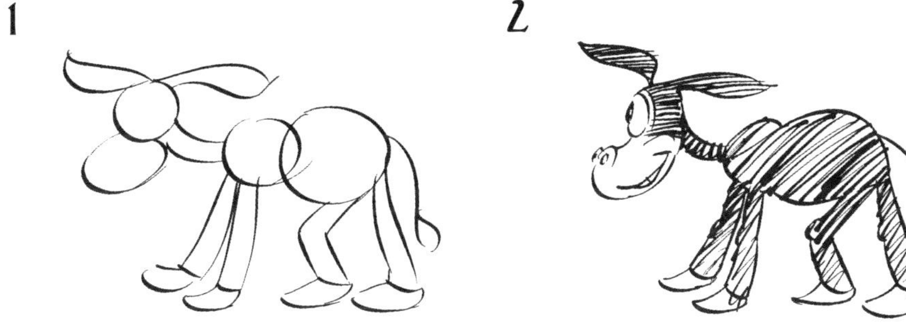

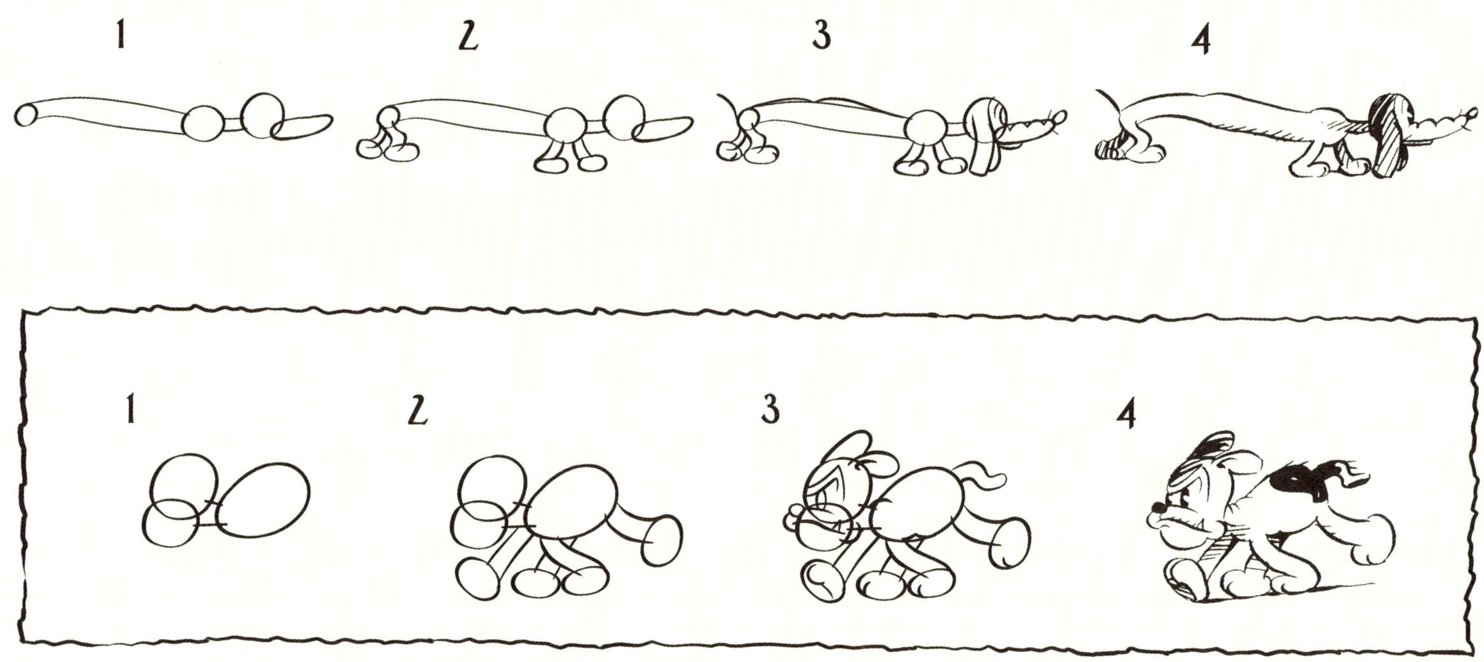
1
2
3
4
1
2
3
4

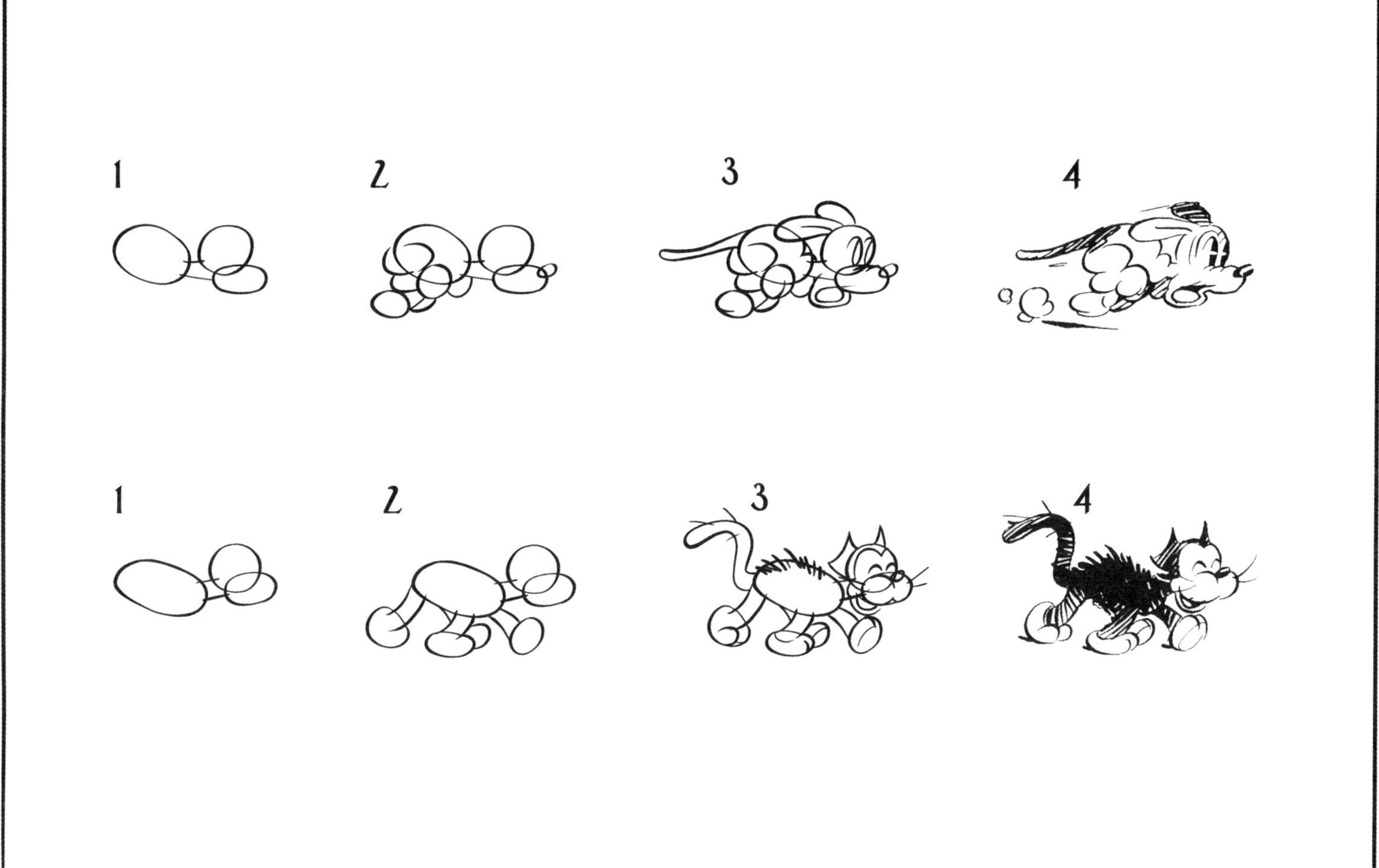

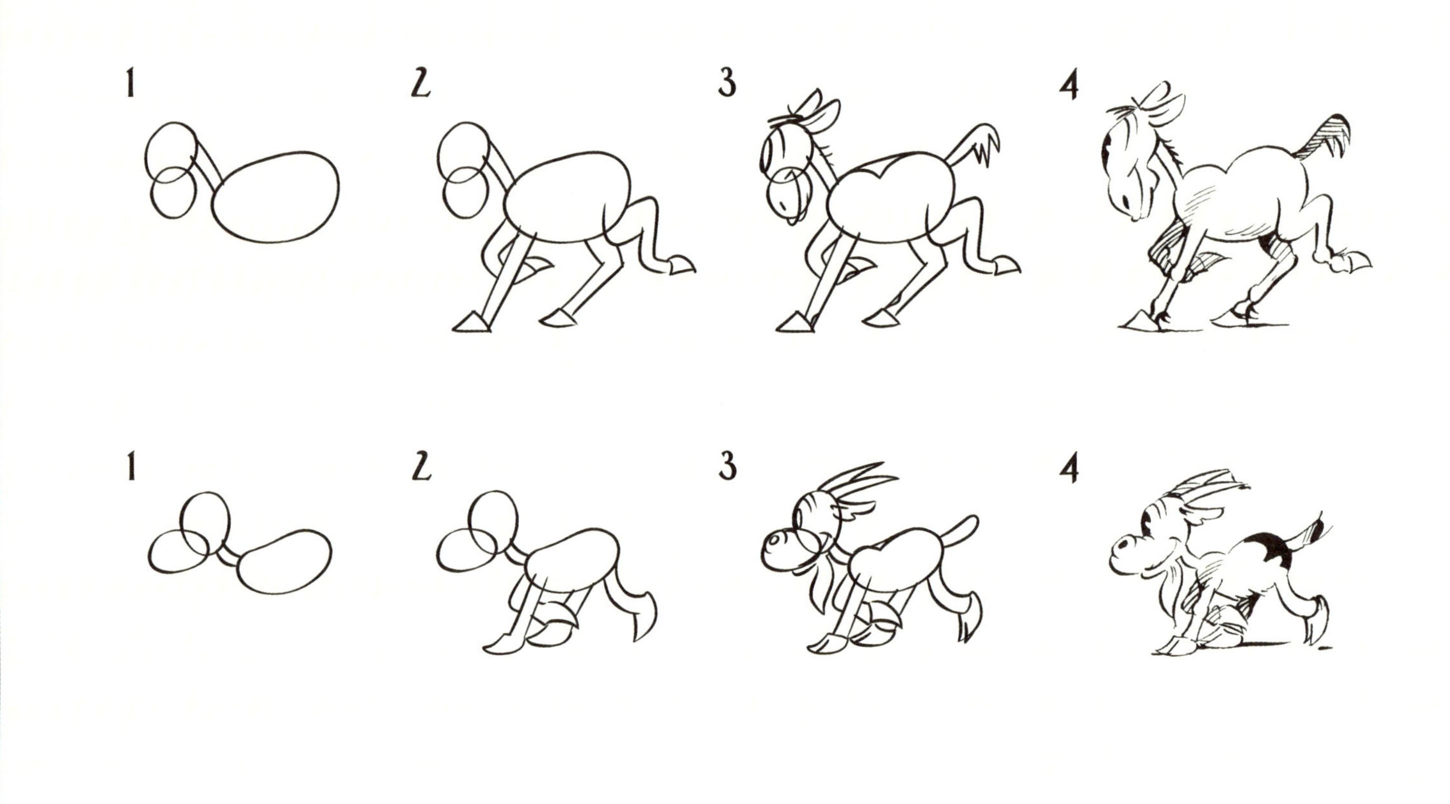
1
2
3
4
1
2
3
4

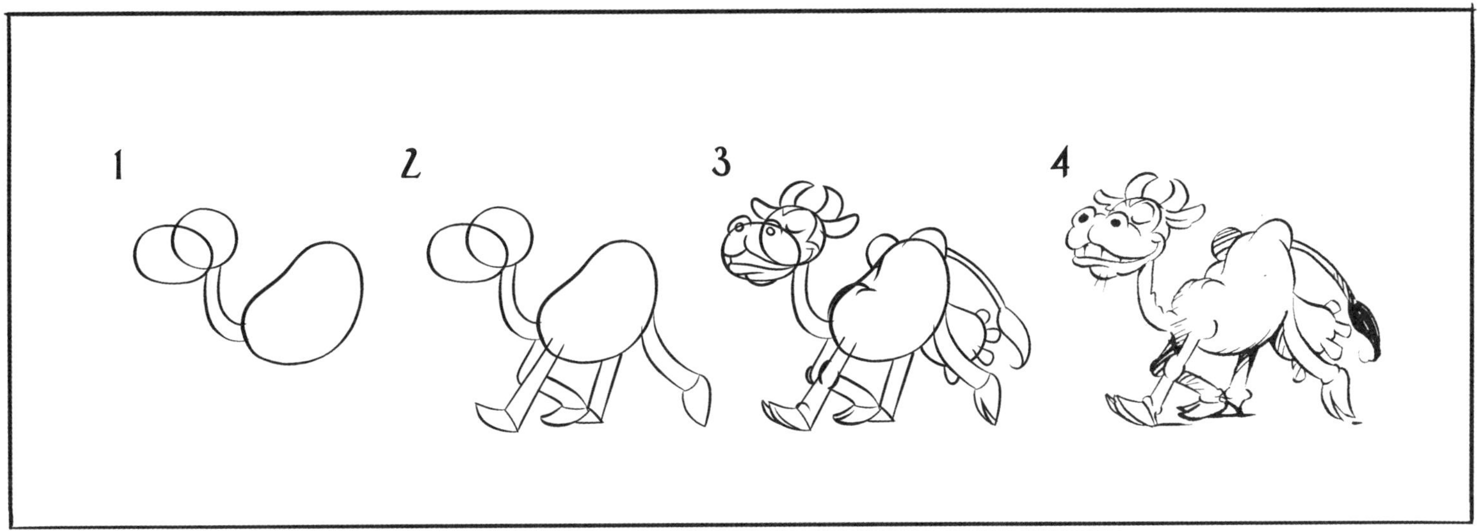

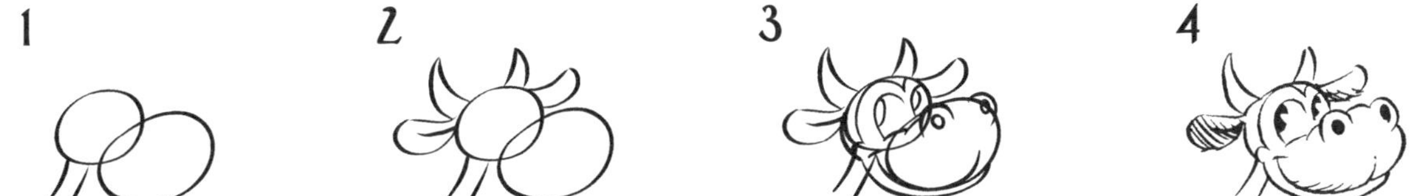
1
2
3
4

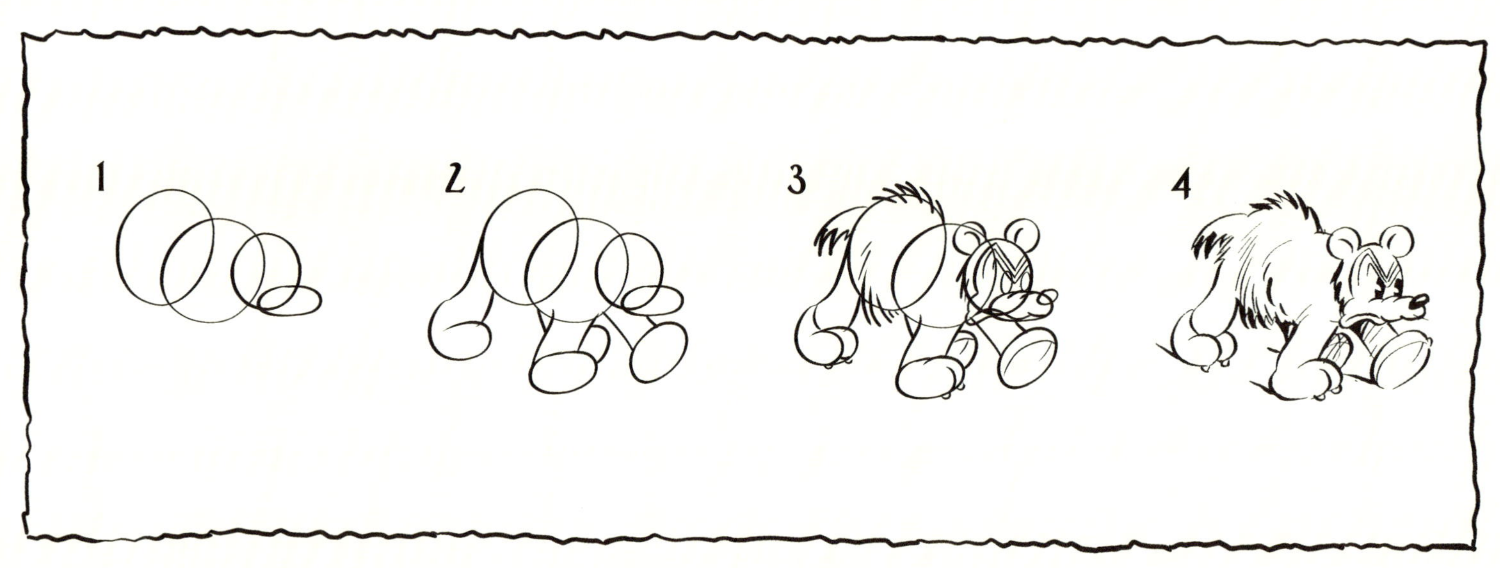
1
2
3
4

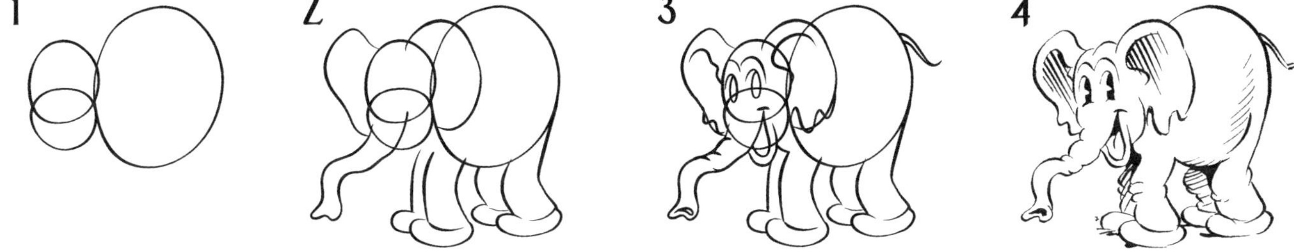

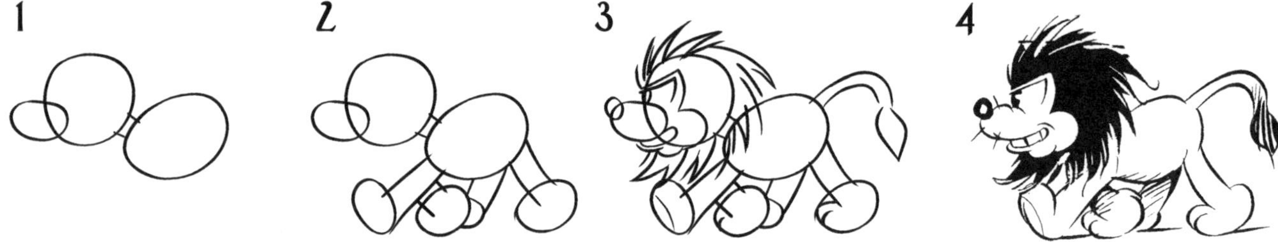

1
2
3
4

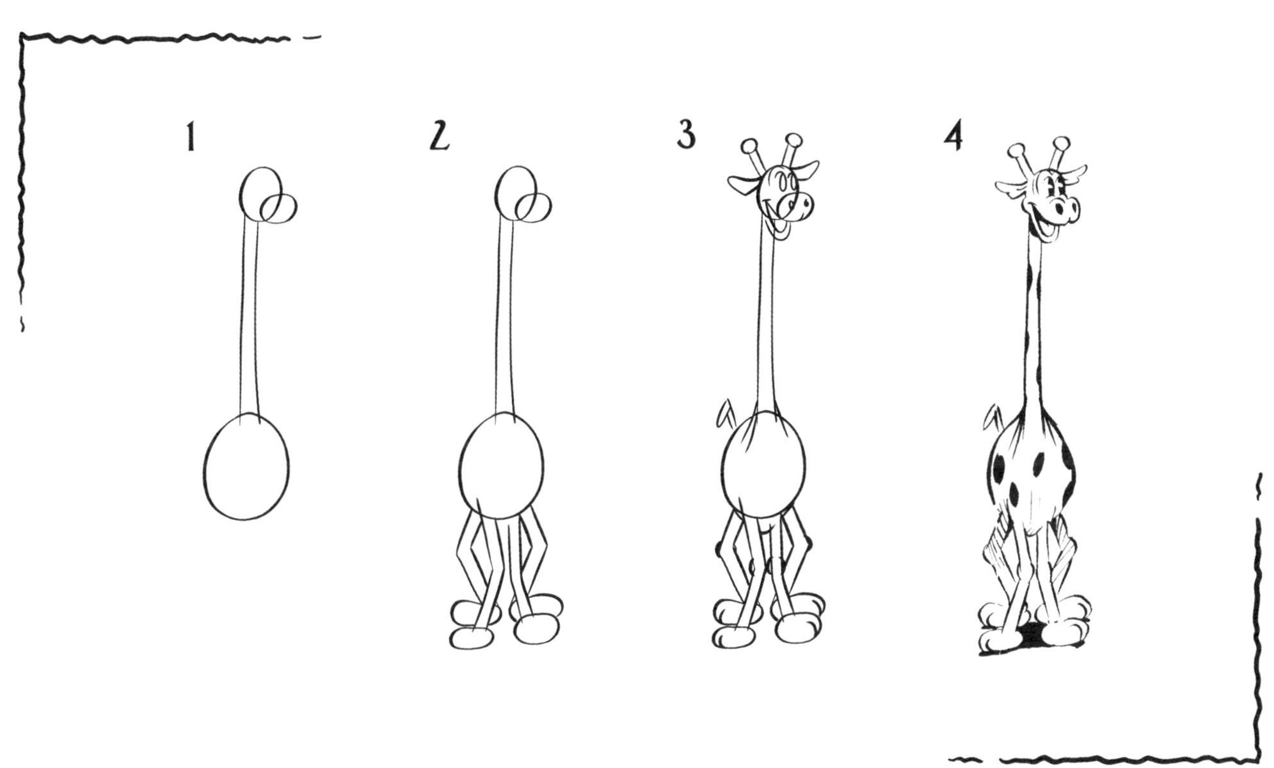

1
2
3
4

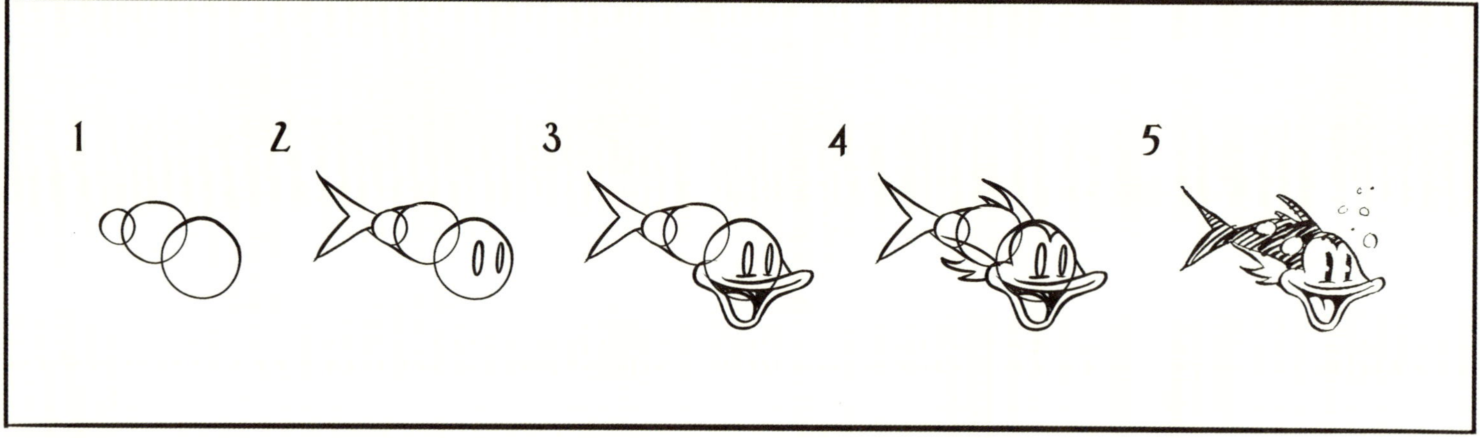

1
2
3
4
5

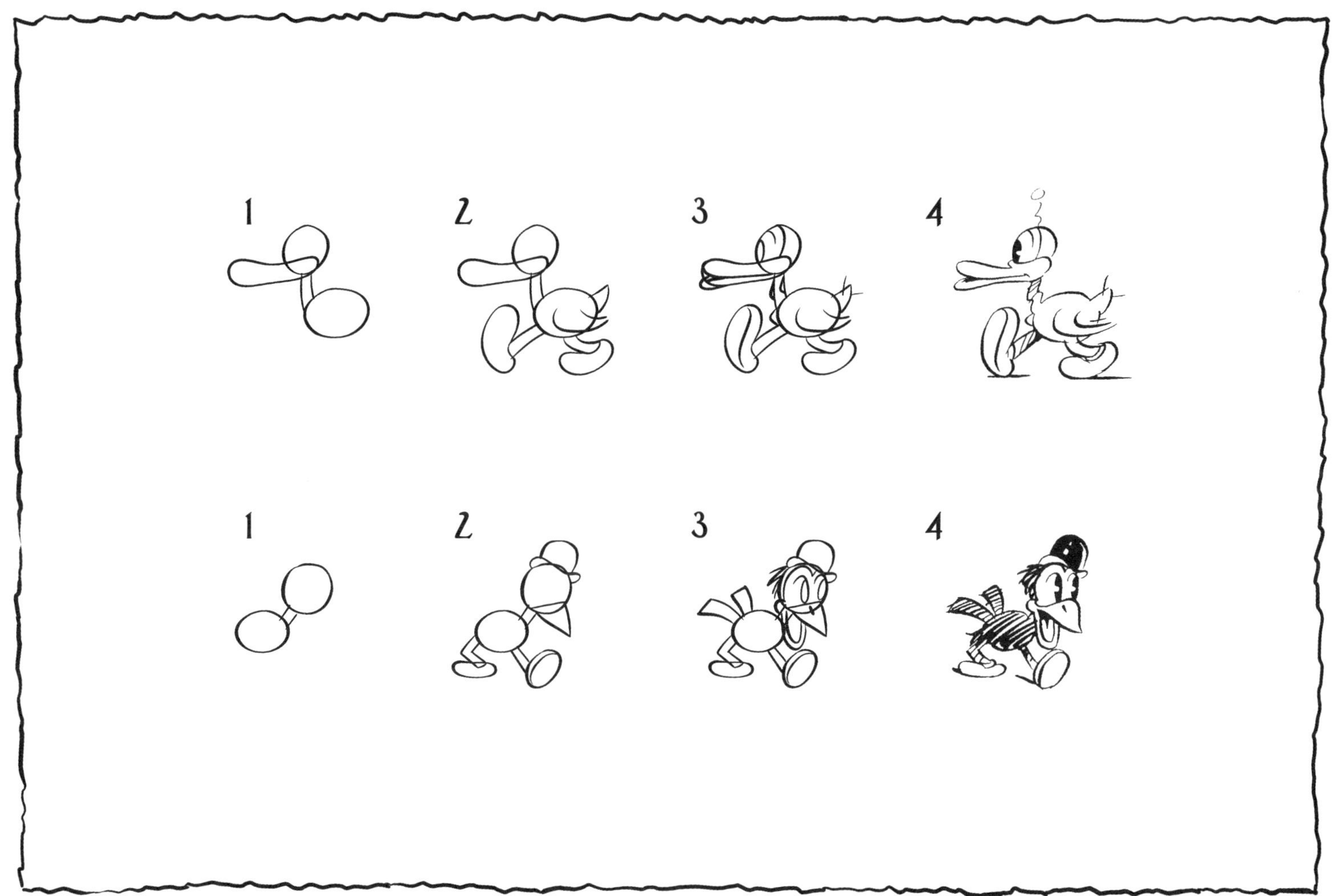
1
2
3
4
1
2
3
4

Conclusion

There is no end to what you can do if you get firmly fixed in
your mind the idea of building comics from the basic circles.

The system of drawing comics, presented in this book, is one
used by the famous motion-picture cartoonists in creating their
laughter-provoking characters for the screen. They have made
comic art pay big dividends; but only by hard work
and practice.

Comic art will do the same for you once you master it.
This you can do only by diligent practice.

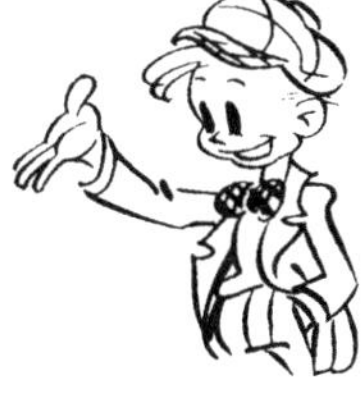

Illustrations by Bill Nolan and Walter Newton
Edited by Gary Panton
Designed by Zoe Bradley
Cover designed by Moesha Kellaway

Manufacturer: First published in Great Britain in 2025 by LOM ART, an imprint of Michael O'Mara Books Limited, 9 Lion Yard, Tremadoc Road, London SW4 7NQ
www.mombooks.com

Represented by: Authorised Rep Compliance Ltd, Ground Floor, 71 Lower Baggot Street, Dublin D02 P593, Ireland
www.arccompliance.com

 www.mombooks.com/lom   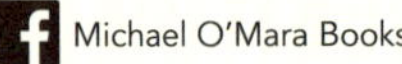 Michael O'Mara Books    @lomart.books

Some material in this book was originally published in *Cartooning Self-Taught* in 1936.
This edition copyright © Michael O'Mara Books Limited 2025

A CIP catalogue record for this book is available from the British Library.

ISBN: 978-1-915751-35-5

1 3 5 7 9 10 8 6 4 2

This product is made of material from well-managed, FSC®-certified forests and other controlled sources. The manufacturing processes conform to the environmental regulations of the country of origin.

Printed in Dubai, UAE.

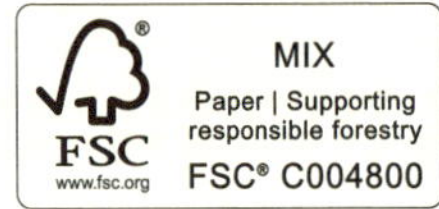

For further information see www.mombooks.com/about/sustainability-climate-focus
Report any safety issues to product.safety@mombooks.com